the great B̶ Pepper COOKBOOK

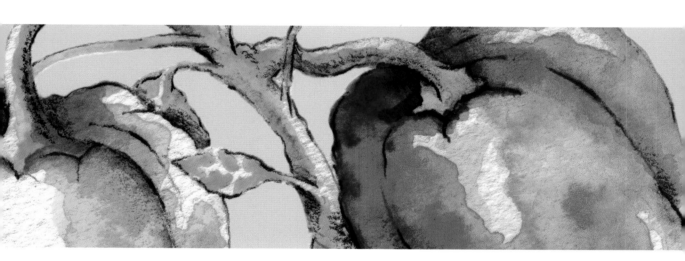

Published in 2014 by Libri Publishing ■ Copyright © Libri Publishing ■ ISBN: Paperback 978 0 9930002 1 8 ■ All rights reserved. No part of this publication may be reproduced, stored in any retrieval system or transmitted in any form or by any means, electronic, mechanical, photocopying, recording or otherwise, without the prior written permission of the copyright holder for which application should be addressed in the first instance to the publishers. No liability shall be attached to the author, the copyright holder or the publishers for loss or damage of any nature suffered as a result of reliance on the reproduction of any of the contents of this publication or any errors or omissions in its contents. ■ A CIP catalogue record for this book is available from The British Library ■ Design by Helen Taylor ■ Cover Illustration by Nicky Storr ■ Printed in the UK by Berforts Information Press ■ Redshank Books, an imprint of Libri Publishing, Brunel House, Volunteer Way, Faringdon, Oxfordshire SN7 7YR ■ Tel: +44 (0)845 873 3837 ■ www.libripublishing.co.uk

the great British Pepper COOKBOOK

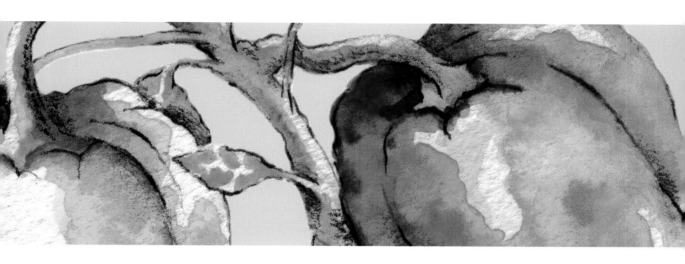

Edited by
Liz O'Keefe

REDSHANK
BOOKS

Contents

Foreword by Gary Taylor MBE 7

Welcome from the editor 9

Think you know peppers? 10

A peppered history 11

Peppers under the microscope 13

Health and nutrition 17

The great British pepper growers 19

Preparing peppers 17

Easy Pepper Recipes

Vietnamese pepper salad (V) 28

Sweet pepper salmon (gf) 31

Thai turkey and pepper stir-fry 32

Herby pepper and halloumi kebabs (V) (gf) 33

Pan-fried seabass with pepper and paprika sauce (gf) 34

Roast pepper couscous (V) 35

Barbecued pepper melts (V) (gf) 36

Hot guacamole (V) (gf) 38

Berry and red pepper smoothie (V) (gf) 39

Chilli hot chocolate (V) 40

Spicy tofu and noodle soup (V) 41

Steamed Vietnamese stuffed peppers 42

Virgin pepper Mary (V) (gf) 44

Salsa salu (V) (gf) 45

Goat's cheese, walnut and chicory salad
with yellow pepper dressing (V) (gf) 46

Gazpacho (V) (gf) 47

Chorizo, yellow pepper and basil penne 43

Recipes with a Little Extra Effort

Mixed pickled peppers (V) (gf) 50

Red pepper, feta and mint muffins (V) 52

Brazilian black bean soup (gf) 54

Pepper balti (V) 56

Orange pepper cheesecake 58

Red pepper and cream cheese cupcakes 59

Roast tomato and red pepper relish (V) (gf) 60

Hearty meatballs   61

Pepper, aubergine and goat's cheese tart (V)   62

Jambalaya (gf)   64

Madagascar chicken (gf)   65

Chilli and red pepper chocolate mousse (gf)   66

African sunrise salad (V)   69

Puppy breath chilli   70

Peperonata (V) (gf)   71

Thai green crab curry (gf)   72

Chicken and pepper risotto (gf)   73

Beef stroganoff   74

Red pepper pasta (V)   75

Lamb sosaties (gf)   76

Posh Pepper Recipes

Beef and pepper Wellington   80

Sweet potato, roasted pepper and chorizo loaf   82

Mini pepper and vegetable tempura with
sweet chilli sauce (V)   84

Moroccan mutton and pepper tagine   85

Seafood and peppers in black bean sauce   86

Scottish pepper, potato and black pudding breakfast stack   88

Stuffed padron peppers (Bharela Marcha) (V) (gf)   89

Red pepper damper bread (V)   90

Seared lamb, lentil and roasted red pepper salad
with salsa verde   91

Squash and pepper stacks (V) (gf)   92

Fried squid with romesco sauce and pepper croutons   93

Tofu and spinach stuffed pepper curry (V) (gf)   94

Beef and pepper bunny chow   96

Fillet steak with pepper cream sauce (gf)   97

Red pepper, lemon and coriander focaccia (V)   98

Roasted lamuyo pepper with chorizo and
garlic toast tapas   99

Rare tuna 'au poivre' and piperade tapas (gf)   100

About the Pepper Technology Group   103

Contributors   104

Meet the growers   106

Index   109

(gf) recipes may be 'served with' an accompaniment that includes gluten

GARY TAYLOR MBE
Chairman and founder of the PTG
(Pepper Technology Group), chairman
of the LVGA (Lea Valley Growers
Association), HDC protected edible
panel and HDC Board member. Gary
is a director of Valley Grown Nurseries
in Nazeing, Essex and has extensive
knowledge of the fresh food industry,
which he has worked in for over forty
years. Valley Grown Nurseries donated
the Beef stroganoff recipe found on
page 74. Gary was awarded an MBE for
services to the Pepper Industry in the
2013 Honours List.

Foreword by Gary Taylor MBE

Welcome to the Pepper Technology Group's *The Great British Pepper Cookbook*.

The group represents most of the sweet pepper growers in the United Kingdom as well as a number of chilli growers.

The group started from humble beginnings in 2003 with two grower members, one sponsor and two representatives from the HDC (Horticultural Development Council, now company). In 2014 we now boast eighteen grower members, thirteen sponsors and three HDC representatives covering technical, communications and crop protection.

We are a proactive, non-profit making organisation that looks to engage with the public on various levels either through our website, at local and national shows and more recently at an event in the Houses of Parliament to celebrate National Salad Awareness Day. Our primary aim is to promote our world class and varied produce to a wider audience.

The Great British Pepper Cookbook is filling a gap in the cookbook market as there seems little that has gone before. By informing the reader on the history, nutrition, growing techniques and the diverse nature of growing peppers we hope to set ourselves apart from a normal cookbook.

My thanks to Redshank Books for publishing the book, to the Lea Valley Growers Association in part, marking its centenary celebration by sponsoring the book, and to Media Street Ltd. To Neal Ward (Dr Pepper) for his considerable contributions to the book. Without him I would have lost my sanity or what was left of it when we started this journey three years ago.

My final thanks goes to Liz O'Keefe who has turned what was a good book into something that we are all rightly proud of. We could not have achieved what we have without her knowledge, drive and passion for all things peppers.

Many thanks to all who have played their part, however great or small, in this journey from what was a simple idea to now being a firm reality.

We hope you enjoy the rich and varied recipes presented to you in this, *The Great British Pepper Cookbook*.

Gary Taylor MBE
Chairman of PTG

LIZ O'KEEFE

A qualified chef, ex-horticultural journalist, recipe developer and food and drinks writer, Liz O'Keefe has brought all of her experience and flair for both growing and cookery to *The Great British Pepper Cookbook*.

Liz travelled all over the UK and the world reporting on fresh produce production, as part of five years writing for business magazine *Fresh Produce Journal* and is no stranger to the British pepper industry.

A judge of many an award, including the Guild of Fine Foods' Great Taste Awards and the World Bread Awards, she is the creator of recipe-led website Seasonal Dinner Parties, a chef on the Good Food Channel website and is a former cookery editor of national monthly consumer food magazine *eat in*.

Welcome from the editor

Here is *The Great British Pepper Cookbook* and all you'll ever need to know about growing, cooking and eating peppers. Like the British pepper industry itself, this book has taken the time and knowledge of such a lot of experienced and enthusiastic people – with just a pinch and a bit of that pepper passion (it will get you in the end). Just ask Gary Taylor. When head of the Pepper Technology Group, Gary approached me to put together this amalgamation of pepper history, growing, nutritional information and recipes on behalf of the group, it was clear that this was a lively industry just waiting to get out from behind its closed glasshouse doors.

Having spent time writing on the sidelines of the fresh produce industry, it has been great to see the pepper growing industry increase the amount of peppers they grow, continue to keep their top-notch glasshouses in optimum condition and bring interesting types of peppers, such as the mini sweet pepper and the pointed pepper to our dinner tables. But, as a nation, do we fully utilize this in the kitchen? Peppers are celebrated (and consumed an awful lot more) in other countries. So for this book, I have grabbed culinary inspiration from around the world, as well as featuring recipe contributions from food writers and chef friends from all walks of the cookery scene.

Our recipe pages will have you making an array of exotic recipes, from Vietnamese pho to Brazilian black bean soup, as well as more traditional British fodder like Beef (pepper) Wellington and Pepper, aubergine and goat's cheese tart. It will also serve as a bit of a skill glossary in the kitchen, with instructions on how to make pastries, stocks, breads and pasta, as well as how to cook the perfect steak and get that poached egg just right.

Along with comprehensive information about the pepper industry that will fill any dinner party or supper with food for thought, this little book is all you need to help those tasty British peppers shine whether it be breakfast or lunch, a quick snack or an impressive feast.

We hope you enjoy the pepper journey as much as we did,

Liz and the Pepper Team

Think you know peppers?

Peppers: think again…

What are peppers? If you think they are the things you chop up for a salad or stuff for vegetarians, then it's time to think again. Officially, according to those knowledgeable scientists out there, peppers are actually a fruit. Like a lot of products that are sold as salad products, such as tomatoes and cucumbers, peppers have seed-containing bodies produced by the plant as part of its sexual reproduction, deeming them fruit. Too much? Yes, let's have less of that.

Going back to the fruit issue though, one of the main reasons the magnificent pepper gets neglected in our kitchens in the UK is that it is a fruit that has stuck in our minds as a salad. It's like people treating avocados as a fruit rather than a vegetable (Let's pass on that fruit salad) and how sad would it be to live in a world where we used tomatoes for salads only? The answer is: very.

So, let us start at the beginning: how does a pepper grow? Well, pepper seeds once traditionally consumed and distributed elsewhere straight from the pepper by herbivorous animals, are now more likely to be propagated into young shoots by horticulturalists and later planted in a glasshouse. Pepper flowers form at junction points on the stem and, if successfully pollinated by bees in warm and light conditions, go on to form fruit. A commercial grower will have ripe peppers ready to harvest after a couple of months, with green peppers being picked just before ripeness and red peppers staying on the vine for the longest, with the final colour depending on the variety.

Pick a pepper

With any fruit or veg, it's best to get the freshest you can and choose what you cook with wisely.

Look: A fresh pepper should be bright, whatever its colour, and have a green, fresh-looking stem. Its skin should not majorly wrinkled and hydrated, and should have a shiny appearance. Go for a pepper Vidal Sassoon would be proud of.

Touch: Pick up a pepper and give it a gentle squeeze — not too much; other people may want it. The thick flesh of a really fresh blocky bell pepper won't give too much. Pointed peppers will always be a little softer, even when they are fresh because of their thinner flesh. Fruit should feel quite heavy for their size.

To use a pepper to its full versatile, culinary potential, first we need to understand what it has been through to survive history and maintain its place on our dinner tables.

A peppered history

Thought to originate in Bolivia, peppers are now grown widely on every continent of the world, except Antarctica. As either a vegetable or flavouring ingredient, they form a major part of the diet in numerous cuisines around the world, especially in tropical regions, where they can be grown in open fields year round. Rather ahead of the culinary times, South American countries have used peppers since 7500 BC, whereas Europeans have only been eating peppers for the last 500 years, when they were introduced as fantastical new plants alongside tomatoes, potatoes and tobacco by explorers like Columbus and Drake in the 1400s and 1500s.

In their quest to find sources of exotic spices in the Far East, Spanish explorers travelled westward and stumbled upon both sweet and hot peppers. Being tropical plants, peppers became widely cultivated in areas such as India, and hot chillies replaced peppercorns in many recipes. It is thought that cultivated peppers moved from the orient, through the Ottoman Empire and into the cuisine of Eastern Europe, where 'paprika', either in fresh form as long mildly spicy varieties, or as a dried ground (and often smoked) powder, is now a major ingredient of numerous dishes. At the same time as peppers were being cultivated along the spice trade routes to and from Europe, they also became popular in warmer Mediterranean countries. From Southern Europe, the use of capsicums is thought to have spread northwards, reaching England in the mid–16th century.

Back then, a pepper had a long way to go to get to our tables, with another long journey to make after going along the spice trade route over the English Channel. With no fancy freight containers or technologies to help them, peppers probably made their appearance in a pickled form. The well-known English nursery rhyme tongue twister 'Peter Piper picked a peck of pickled peppers' pays homage to this and was first published in 1813. (A peck is a traditional unit of volume, equivalent to two gallons or around nine litres.)

In the 19th century, recipes began appearing in a number of American and British cookbooks, such as *The Practical Cook Book* by Mrs. Bliss (1850), *Buckeye Cookery and Practical Housekeeping* by Estelle Woods Wilcox (1877), *The Curry Cook's Assistant; or Curries, how to make them in England in their original Style* by D. Santiagoe (1889), Cassell's New Universal Cookery Book by Lizzie Heritage (1894).

See page 50 for the Mixed pickled peppers recipe

Peppers under the microscope

Variety is the spice of life

Are you ready for a bit more science? Let's go. Even though the **capsicum genus** plant has approximately 30 known species, only five of these are actually fully utilized and in common use. The **capsicum annuum** (meaning annual) is the largest domesticated species and includes the standard bell pepper, jalapeño, poblano/ancho, serrano, cayenne, peperoncini and anaheim/NuMex peppers. The annuum also includes some of the more unique pepper varieties, such as the unusual Peter Pepper and Bolivian Rainbow. The **capsicum baccatum** (meaning berry-like) is an unusual species grown primarily in South America, where it is referred to locally as 'Aji'. This species includes such pepper varieties Aji Amarillo, Aji Colorado, Aji Andean and Lemon Drop. The **capsicum chinense** means 'from China', which is rather misleading as they originated in the Amazon, and includes some of the world's hottest peppers – habanero, Scotch bonnet, datil, fatalii, and Billy Goat, to name a few. Most peppers in this species are extremely hot, with one notable exception of the Aji Dulce, which has the habanero flavour, but with little or no heat. The **capsicum frutescens** (meaning bushy) includes few commercial grown varieties, but includes the peppers that make Tabasco Sauce, as well as the Zimbabwe Bird Pepper, Cambodian Angkor Sunrise and Brazilian Malagueta. **Capsicum pubescens**, which means hairy, are rare peppers characterized by furry leaves, as well as unusually shaped black or dark brown seeds unique to this particular species, and includes Peruvian Rocotos, Bolivian Locotos and Mexican Manzanos.

See page 56 for the Pepper balti recipe, which uses mini sweet peppers

The genus capsicum belongs to the nightshade family of flowering plants and many members of this family contain chemicals called alkaloids, of which one is capsaicin – the hot taste in chillies. The Scoville scale, developed in 1912 by American pharmacist Wilbur Scoville, describes the hotness of peppers and is still used by breeders and growers worldwide. And, in a big plus point for scientists, modern day laboratory equipment now means we can measure the amount of capsaicin in a pepper rather than relying on human taste buds. To give you a bit of an idea, pure capsaicin stands at 16 million Scoville heat units (SHU), a bird's eye chilli is 50,000–100,000 SHU and the bell pepper is right at the other end of the scale at zero SHU.

Thanks to commercial horticultural breeding, there are many different varieties within each species, each with their own unique shape, flavour and colours. The most common peppers used are:

Bell Pepper

The most widely used pepper in the UK, the bell pepper, also known as sweet pepper or capsicum, is a blocky, bell-shaped fruit at around 10 to 15cm high and 8 to 10cm wide, with three or four lobes. Bell peppers can be a wide range of different colours from the classic red, yellow, orange and green, to the more unusual purple, brown, black and white.

Sweet Pointed Pepper

Often referred to as 'Ramiro' or 'Romano', these have a similarly sweet flavour, but the flesh is thinner and flavours are more concentrated. They have been grown in the UK for the past decade or so and are generally only available in the UK as ripe red, orange or yellow fruit, but green ones are available in other parts of the world.

Mini Sweet Pepper

Looking rather like Scotch bonnet chillies or a mini bell pepper, these baby peppers have no heat and are intensely sweet. Grown in the UK for the past decade or so, they have proven popular as snacking peppers and with children. They are also known as Sweet Bite.

Cubanelle

These chilli-looking peppers are common in Southern Europe and America and fried and stuffed in recipes. Not widely available in UK shops, the cubanelle lies somewhere between a sweet pepper and a chilli, with a very mild spiciness. The variety is long and narrow and the peppers are usually sold when an unripe light green/yellow colour.

Banana Pepper

Also known as the yellow wax pepper, the banana pepper is a mild chilli pepper around 5–8cm long and has a curved shape. Banana peppers are usually yellow, but can ripen to orange or red.

Cayenne Pepper

Around 12–15cm in length, these chilli peppers are commonly dried and ground to be used as a spice. Cayenne peppers vary in colour from dark green to red, yellow and orange.

Habanero

The Habanero is an extremely hot chilli pepper, with an average of 200,000 to 300,000 Scoville heat units. Around 2–6cm long and available in a wide array of different colours, the Habanero should be used with caution.

Bird's Eye

These Mexican chillies, sometimes known as Thai chillies, are small and tapered, and come in either red or green, and sometimes yellow. Often used in Chinese and South East Asian cooking, it is a cultivar from the annuum and commonly found in Southeast Asia. Widely used in the UK, this little chilli features in quite a few recipes in this book.

Jalapeño

Popular pickled, the jalapeño is a medium-sized chilli pepper at around 7cm long. Although usually picked and eaten in its green state, the jalapeño can be allowed to ripen to red. A cracked skin, referred to as 'corking', on a jalapeño is often considered an indicator of spiciness.

Pimento

Available in both green and red, the pimento pepper is slightly more aromatic than the bell pepper and can be used as a substitute. Pimentos are heart shaped and around 7–10cm long.

Scotch Bonnet

Similar to the Habanero in terms of heat and slightly smaller in size, the Scotch bonnet pepper is widely used in Caribbean cuisine. This is another chilli pepper that should be used with caution, so be sure to wash your hands after handling!

Serrano

Serrano chilli peppers are one of the most popular chillies in Mexico and notably hotter than the jalapeño pepper. They are red to green in colour, with a glossy exterior and around 6cm long.

Tabasco

Tabasco peppers, named after the Mexican state of Tabasco, measure 1–2cm in length and 3–7mm in diameter and can be yellow-green, yellow, orange or red in colour.

Bhut Jolokia

Sometimes known as naga jolokia, ghost pepper or red naga chilli, this pepper is grown in India and is an interspecies hybrid of mostly chinense with some frutescens genes. It was the world's hottest pepper in 2007 and 401.5 times hotter than Tabasco sauce, rating at more than 1 million SHUs.

Trinidad Moruga Scorpion

Native to the district of Moruga in Trinidad and Tobago, the Trinidad Moruga Scorpion has a heat of more than 1.2 million SHUs. It looks like a tiny version of a bell pepper and similar to a Scotch bonnet, although it is very wrinkled.

Carolina Reaper

The Carolina Reaper is a hybrid cultivar of chilli pepper of the chinense species and a cross between a red naga pepper and a red savina pepper. It has a 2.2 million SHU and was rated as the world's hottest chilli pepper by Guinness World Records in 2012.

Serrano, jalapeño, bird's eye, habanero, cayenne, cubanelle, bell and banana pepper pictures courtesy of recipetips.com

Health and nutrition

Let's start with the real news: red and yellow peppers have four times as much vitamin C as oranges. An 80g portion of raw red or yellow pepper (about a pepper and a half) gives you approximately 200% of your recommended daily allowance, and it doesn't get your fingers all sticky.

That's not all on the vitamin front, all peppers – no matter what colour they are – include the vitamins Bl, B6, E, and K, as well as minerals like potassium, magnesium and iron. It seems that yellow peppers can give carrots a run for their money as they also contain significant amounts of lutein and zeaxanthin, which is important for healthy eyesight. And, there are no surprise large amounts of fat or calories when it comes to our trusty peppers – there are just 15 calories per 100g in a green pepper.

So, let's break this down per 100g (or a couple of slices to crunch on). In the green corner, we have 15 calories, 2.6g carbohydrates, 0.3g fat, 1.6g fibre and 0.8g protein. Team yellow has 26 calories, 5.3g carbohydrates, 0.2g fat, 1.7g fibre and 1.2g protein, and the reds deliver 32 calories, 6.4g carbohydrates, 0.4g fat, 1.6g fibre and 1g protein.

Children with asthma can also benefit from eating peppers and studies have shown that a diet high in Vitamin C can significantly reduce wheezing among young sufferers. The fabulous antioxidant lycopene, which works hard to reduce the risk of some forms of cancer and cardiovascular disease, is the stuff that gives red peppers and chillies their colour. In fact, capsaicin has also been linked to cancer prevention, reduced cholesterol and raised endorphin levels, as well as appetite suppression.

Putting the strings up for the new plants

Placing new plants placed out on the slabs

Fixing the first string to support the plant

Stringing the first plants

A sea of yellow

Yellow peppers ready for transport

The great British pepper growers

What's the secret to a good pepper? A quietly run professional structure of experienced and highly technologically advanced growers and growing facilities mainly throughout South England, from Essex to Sussex, to Kent and Hertfordshire, working to produce fruit consistently for 10 months of the year, day in day out.

Water works

Reliant on high light levels (that's bright weather, to you and me), heat and moisture, peppers are harvested from February and November in the UK and are grown in mighty glasshouses that have to be run as tight ships. British growers mainly use soil-less hydroponic systems. The word hydroponics comes from the Greek for water (hydro) and work (ponos) and that's exactly what the growing system means – it makes the water work to its full ability to produce the most product to land in the most efficient way.

In fact, UK growers produce 28 million tonnes of peppers a year, because of these effective hydroponic systems, which allow them to grow larger fruit and produce more of it. Coming complete with computer programmes that adjust components like temperature, feed and oxygen, the pepper plants grow into slabs of growing material like rockwool or coco fibre, where the roots get lots of oxygen and can be fed with a specially formulated nutrient solution via a tank. Any feed that is not taken up by the crop runs down the gutters on which the plants grow and back to a holding tank, meaning nothing goes to waste. This special formula provides all the minerals and nutrients required for a healthy plant, traditionally supplied by soil, which can carry diseases and harmful pests. Without soil, growers can keep the growing environment under control, as well as the acidity of the plants and therefore the amount of nutrients the roots take in. The systems allow the growers to control almost every aspect of the plants' root environment and the vines are then trained upwards by holsters that are adjusted according to the growth speed as the plant grows and produces flowers that turn into peppers throughout the vine.

A number of PTG members grow their pepper crops in the soil according to organic principles. No synthetic pesticides or fertiliser are permitted in these crops so these growers must nourish the soil with organic manures and composts and control pests and diseases with a limited range of naturally occurring chemicals and biological agents like bacteria.

Getting hot, hot, hot

We all know how changeable British weather can be and this is a matter forever on pepper growers' minds. Traditionally speaking, glasshouses are heated in the cooler months by natural gas traditional boilers and this is how the British pepper growers started out growing peppers some 35 years ago. The boilers heat water that is then circulated through the glasshouse in pipes to keep the air warm. Plants make carbohydrates (i.e. sugars and starch) from water and CO_2 in the presence of light by the process of photosynthesis and by burning fossil fuels and therefore producing more CO_2, photosynthesis occurs more, meaning bigger plants and more fruit.

Like us humans, pepper plants are nocturnal and only absorb the carbon dioxide in the day. So growers must burn gas during the day, when the heat may not be required. You'll be pleased to know, they don't waste fuel just for the sake of CO_2 though. Unwanted hot water is stored in insulated buffer tanks during the day and pumped back warm into the glasshouse at night.

More recently growers have begun to use combined heat and power systems (CHP). The CHP engines burn gas to generate electricity in addition to the heat and carbon dioxide, making the pepper growing systems even more cost-effective and efficient. A system widely used in the Netherlands, during the day CHP uses hot water in buffer tanks to create and pump CO_2 around the glasshouse and uses gas to produce electricity, which can then be used to power the businesses facilities, as well as be sold back to the national grid. At night, the hot water from the buffer tanks keeps the glasshouse warm. Examples in the UK of this include the 50ha salad growing glasshouse, Thanet Earth, which can produce enough electricity to power its surrounding residential houses in Kent.

The pepper challenge ahead

Efficient use of energy and water is hugely important and will become an even bigger task for British pepper growers in the coming years, as fossil fuels are depleted and the demand for water in the UK increases. In the future, pepper growers hope to make more use of renewable energy sources such as biofuels, and use fewer artificially manufactured fertilisers and pesticides. PTG members are also constantly monitoring water use efficiency and looking at new ways to reduce the water-footprint of each fruit. As well as growing great-tasting, good quality peppers, they are also trying to produce them at a lower cost to the environment.

Wind and solar power are becoming more widely used to generate electricity, however growing glasshouse crops can require considerable amounts of additional heat. Harnessing the power of underground geothermal energy may be possible for some growers, whilst turning plant, food and animal waste into gas through anaerobic bacterial digestion may also be an alternative to natural gas or oil. Biomass burners are already replacing natural gas boilers in some nurseries, and as this technology develops, more and more growers may consider it a viable alternative.

The production of synthetic fertilisers uses large amounts of energy, so reducing our reliance on them can help us produce peppers in a more sustainable way. Animal manures and composted domestic waste are already becoming more common fertilisers for soil-grown crops and these organic forms of nitrogen and phosphorus may be used more in the future as the techniques of applying them in hydroponic crops are developed.

In order to help the plant absorb more nutrients, growers are also using beneficial microbes, like bacteria and fungi, to make the feeding roots more efficient. Scientists are only beginning to really understand how this living mass around the roots can help the plant, but they are working closely with growers to try and harness the power of these microscopic organisms.

Creepy crawlies

Like all intensively grown crops, peppers can easily become overrun with pests that, if they had their way, would eat the flowers and peppers before we'd have the chance to. Growers are striving to use fewer pesticides and instead use naturally occurring methods of pest and disease control whenever possible. Cue the beneficial insects.

Glasshouse crops have been protected from pests by purposely adding natural predators and parasites for a number of decades. By selecting natural enemies that either parasitize or prey on our pests and inundating our crops with them, growers can control most pests without using pesticides. Growers encourage a natural war between the pests and the beneficials, which does not damage the plant themselves.

When pesticides are used it is always the very last resort. Mostly because of the controversy surrounding the products, and because they are so expensive, it just doesn't make good business sense. But neither does losing a complete crop, when one application of an approved chemical can save it. Modern pesticides tend to break down very quickly once they are applied to the plant and many have very specific modes of action that will only kill a specific pest.

Remember, fresh produce grown in Britain is some of the safest in the world. Food hygiene is paramount during the growing, harvesting and packaging of peppers and regular independent inspections of nurseries ensure they are grown safely and take care of the environment at the same time.

Preparing peppers

To quarter: Hold the pepper vertically and slice down from the side of the stalk to the slightly pointed bottom of the pepper, letting your knife glide (see picture 1). Rotate the pepper, repeating the process, cutting into four or five sections (see picture 2) and discard the stalk and seeds. Place the pepper quarters skin-side down and skim the white flesh away from the pepper with a knife, as in picture 3.

To slice, dice or cube: Quarter the peppers, as above, then julienne or sliced peppers can be achieved by cutting the halved pepper section into vertical strips. Then dice the slices into smaller sections or create larger cubes.

To trim: Hold the pepper upright on a chopping board and cut around the stalk by steadily moving the knife and pepper in opposite circular motions to each other (see picture 4), then pull the stalk out carefully (you may want to trim and save it if you are stuffing peppers), trying to remove as many seeds with it as possible, as in picture 5. Remove the further seeds and white flesh by running the knife around the inside of the pepper, being careful not to cut through the pepper wall at all, as in picture 6.

To cut rings: Trim the pepper, as above, and turn the pepper on its side and trim off the top to level (see picture 7). Slice about 1cm thick slices, slowly, making sure the ring stays a consistent thickness all the way down, as in picture 8. It becomes more difficult to cut safely as the uncut section becomes smaller, so be careful of your fingers. Use the end of the pepper (picture 9) chopped or whole in a homemade stock (see page 65).

Tip

You can freeze peppers after preparing – just blanch in boiling water for 2 minutes, then refresh in ice cold water, before drying with kitchen paper and freezing in plastic sandwich bags. Defrost and eat within 3 months.

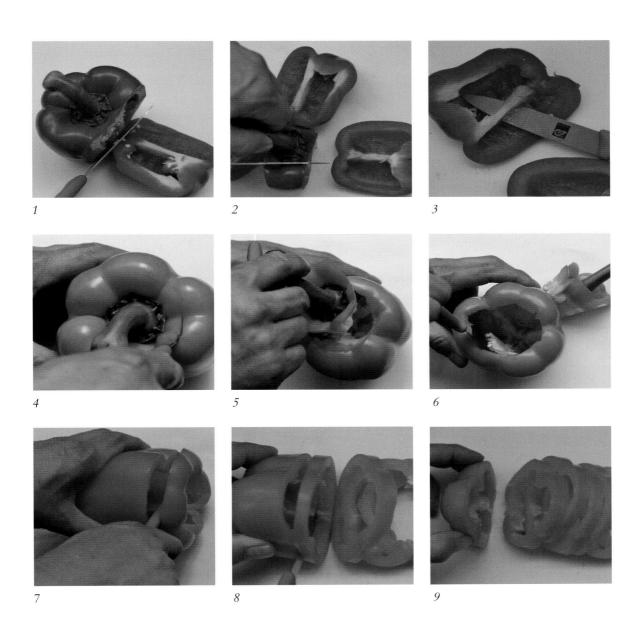

1

2

3

4

5

6

7

8

9

To chop chillies: Some peppers are very spicy, and can linger on your hands and therefore transfer to other sensitive areas very easily. Don't let this put you off as you can get around it very simply. You can wear thin surgical gloves or even washing up rubber gloves or hold the chilli in place while you cut it with a fork instead. Slice the top and stalk off the chilli and cut in half lengthways, as in picture 1. Place the chilli halves skin-side down on a chopping board and scoop out the seeds by running a teaspoon underneath the seeds (see picture 2), close to the chilli exterior. The fleshy pith is what carries the heat or capsaicin of the chilli; the seed also to a lesser extent carries some heat, so leave this in if you want to have a lot of heat in your meal. Wash the chilli halves and slice or dice, as in picture 4. Discard the gloves and wash all the implements and utensils used immediately.

Tip

If you should get any of the chilli on you, rub in vinegar or alcohol on to affected area(s) except the eyes, which should be rinsed with copious amounts of water.

To grill/roast and skin peppers: Preheat the grill, griddle pan, oven or barbecue (some even use a blowtorch – don't preheat that). Follow how to trim a pepper on page 22 and coat with oil. Place the peppers on the grill and cook, turning them for equal cooking, until the skins are blistered (see picture 2). Place in a bowl and cover tightly with cling film or tin foil to seal it, then stand for 15 minutes. The steam will cause the skins to loosen from the peppers and, after 15 minutes, you should be able to peel away the skin completely with ease, as in picture 3. Cut in half lengthways and remove the seeds and fleshy pith.

Tip

Store the cooked peppers, dressed in oil, in a clean, dry jar for up to two days in the fridge. Or freeze them in a sealed airtight bag, and defrost and eat within 3 months.

1

2

3

4

5

6

7

8

9

Pictures 1-4 courtesy of recipetips.com

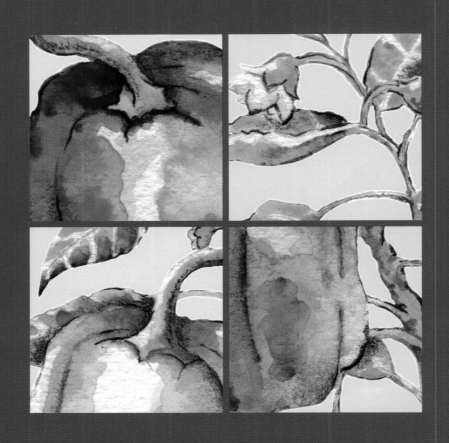

Easy Pepper Recipes

Vietnamese pepper salad (v)

*Raw peppers are great in a salad, but cooked peppers can be even better.
Here, griddling the peppers and then chilling them develops their flavour
and adds a natural sweet and sour element to this salad.*

Serves 2
Ready in 20 minutes, plus standing and chilling

1 Preheat the grill. In a bowl, coat the pepper quarters in the sunflower oil and sprinkle with sugar, then arrange them, skin up, on the grill tray lined with tin foil. Grill until the skins blister, then squeeze the half lemon over them, wrap up in the tin foil and chill for 5 minutes.

2 To make the dressing, mix together the garlic, ginger, sesame seed oil, soy sauce, fish sauce and the chilli with its seeds in a bowl or shake together in a screw-top jar. Chill until needed.

3 In a saucepan, cover the rice noodles with boiling water and stand, off the heat with a lid on, for 5 minutes. Drain and refresh with cold water, until the noodles are cold. Remove the skins from the chilled peppers (they will peel away easily) and slice.

4 In a large serving bowl, mix together the noodles, spring onions, sliced peppers, carrot, cucumber, coriander, mint, peanuts, lime zest and juice and the dressing made in step 2. Stir thoroughly to combine and serve, garnished with the reserved coriander and mint and lime wedges.

Tips

To crush the peanuts, place them in a plastic sandwich bag. Hold the bag together and crush with the end of a rolling pin or jam jar.

You can pick up some very useful julienne cutters (they look similar to vegetable peelers) that will thinly slice your carrots and cucumbers in a jiffy.

4 various colour bell peppers, halved and deseeded

1 tbsp sunflower oil

2 tsp palm or brown sugar

½ lemon

½ clove of garlic, grated

1cm piece fresh root ginger, grated

2 tsp sesame oil

2 tsp soy sauce

1 tsp fish sauce or white vinegar

1 red chilli, very finely slice, reserving the seeds

300g straight-to-wok rice noodles

2 spring onions, trimmed and thinly sliced

1 carrot, cut into thin strips

½ cucumber, cut into thin strips

15g fresh coriander and mint, chopped, reserving some for garnish

1 tbsp unsalted peanuts, slightly crushed

Zest and juice of 1 lime, plus wedges

By Liz O'Keefe

Sweet pepper salmon

This versatile baked salmon dish suits every season. It's also handy to have some cooked and chilled for a salad topping or mixed with natural yogurt and lemon juice as a sandwich filling. You can also try the recipe with other oily fish, like tuna and mackerel.

Serves 4
Ready in 25 minutes

1 Preheat the oven to 190C/gas 5. In a food processor, blend the peppers, oil, sugar, shallots, celery (if using), chilli, vinegar and parsley together, and season. Place the salmon fillets, skin down, in a lightly oiled roasting tray, then coat the fillets with the mixture.

2 Cover with tin foil and bake for 20-25 minutes, until cooked to your liking, removing the foil 5 minutes before the end of cooking. Serve with salad or vegetables and egg noodles or potatoes.

4 red and/or orange bell peppers, deseeded and quartered

2 tbsp olive oil, plus extra for oiling

1 tsp sugar

2 shallots, chopped

1 red chilli, deseeded and chopped

2 celery sticks, chopped (optional)

1 tbsp balsamic vinegar

7g fresh flat leaf parsley, chopped

4 x 250g salmon fillets, skin on

Salt and ground pink peppercorns

By Liz O'Keefe

Thai turkey and pepper stir-fry

This fabulously good for you British Heart Foundation recipe proves turkey is not just for Christmas. Turkey meat is available from spring and then throughout the year, and its stronger taste is a great pairing for peppers. This recipe has only 456 calories, 1.5g of saturated fat, 1.5g salt and 9.3g sugar per portion, making for a balanced, tasty meal and happy hearts.

Serves 4
Ready in 20 minutes

1 In a small bowl, mix the cornflour with 4 tbsp of cold water until smooth. Stir in soy sauce and fish sauce, then set aside. Place the rice in a saucepan and cover with cold water. Bring to the boil then cover with a lid, simmering for 10-12 minutes, until fluffy. Drain and cover.

2 Meanwhile, heat the sunflower oil in a non-stick wok, the stir-fry the red onion, garlic, ginger and chilli over a fairly high heat for 1 minute to release the flavours. Add turkey and continue to stir-fry for 3-4 minutes or until turkey is sealed.

3 Add the red peppers and cook on a slightly lower heat for 2-3 minutes. Mix in the courgette and beansprouts, and stir-fry for 1-2 minutes or until turkey is cooked thoroughly. Stir in the cornflour mixture and cook, stirring, for 1 minute, until the sauce thickens. Stir the coriander and lime juice and zest into the rice, and serve with the stir-fry.

1 tsp cornflour

1 tbsp reduced-sodium soy sauce

2 tsp fish sauce

360g long grain rice, rinsed

2 tsp sunflower oil

1 red onion, thinly sliced

1 clove of garlic, finely chopped

1cm piece fresh root ginger, finely chopped

1 red chilli, deseeded and finely chopped

175g turkey breast strips

2 red bell peppers, deseeded and sliced

1 courgette, cut into matchsticks

55g beansprouts

7g fresh coriander, chopped

Zest and juice of ½ lime

By the British Heart Foundation

Herby pepper and halloumi kebabs (v)

Peppers make a colourful veggie kebab, but why not give meat a rest and welcome this salty, textured cheese, halloumi, into your life as well? These veggie kebabs are perfect for a summer party or make a colourful topping for a salad.

Makes 12
Ready in 20 minutes, plus marinating

1 In a food processor or using a handheld blender and bowl, blend the oil, basil and lemon zest and juice together and season with black pepper. Combine the basil mixture and the halloumi cubes on a plate and chill for at least 15 minutes.

2 Preheat the grill or barbecue. Thread two of each of the halloumi squares, tomatoes, red onion wedges and courgette and pepper slices onto the 12 skewers. Cook on a barbecue for 10–15 minutes or under a preheated grill for 5–10 minutes, turning a few times. Serve two each with salad and jacket potatoes or as on their own as party food.

4 tbsp olive oil

15g fresh basil, chopped

Zest and juice of 1 lemon

500g halloumi, chopped into 24 chunks

24 cherry tomatoes

1 red onion, cut into wedges

2 courgettes, chopped into 24 chunks

3 various colour bell peppers, sliced

Black pepper

You will also need:
12 wooden skewers, soaked in water for 20 minutes and drained

Tip

Make sure all the ingredients are cut to same size so the kebabs cook evenly.

Pan-fried seabass with pepper and paprika sauce

Seabass is one of the best fish to pan fry. It is low in fat to start off with, and so can take the extra oil, and its natural oils develop and sweeten during cooking. Coupled with this Spanish-style sweet pepper sauce, you'll have dinner guests coming round again and again.

Serves 4
Ready in 15 minutes

1 In a food processor or with a hand-held blender, liquidize the peppers and garlic until smooth. Pass the purée through a sieve so that only the juice remains and put that juice into saucepan and simmer until reduced to around a tenth. Stir in the sherry, paprika and seasoning, and then simmer for 2 minutes.

2 Meanwhile, brush the seabass fillets with the olive oil on both sides and season with a pinch of salt. Heat a large frying pan until very hot then add the seabass fillets skin-side down. Cook for 1-2 minutes on each side, until cooked through.

3 Steam the spinach in a steamer or microwave with 2 tsp of water, until wilted, then drain and grate in the nutmeg. Divide the spinach between four plates and sit a seabass fillet on each, then cover with equal amounts of the sauce. Drizzle with oil and serve with mashed potato.

6 red bell peppers, deseeded and chopped

1 clove of garlic, crushed

50ml sherry

1 tsp paprika

4 seabass fillets

4 tbsp olive oil, plus extra for drizzle

600g spinach

1 tsp freshly grated nutmeg

Sea salt and black pepper

Mashed potato, to serve

Roast pepper couscous (v)

Roasting peppers brings out a mellow sweet taste in the fruit and mixes with couscous perfectly. Serve this dish straightaway or chilled, with cubes of feta cheese or roast chicken to make a meal or as an accompaniment to the Moroccan mutton and pepper tagine recipe on page 85

Serves 4
Ready in 20 minutes

1 Preheat the oven to 200C/gas 6. Place the pepper quarters, skin-side up, in a roasting tin and drizzle with half the oil, and season with salt and pepper. Roast for 5-10 minutes, until softened.

2 In a large saucepan, dry-fry the cumin, cloves, ginger, cardamom, coriander and allspice over a medium heat for 30 seconds, or until fragrant.

3 Stir in the remaining oil and onions, and cook for 3-4 minutes, until softened, then add the chilli, orange zest, chickpeas, sultanas, orange juice and vegetable stock. Bring to the boil then add the couscous. Cover and remove from the heat, then stand for 5 minutes. Chop the roasted peppers and mix into the couscous, along with the mint and pinenuts. Serve.

Tip

For an extra fruity dish, add a handful of chopped dried apricots.

2 red and yellow bell peppers, deseeded and quartered

2 tbsp olive oil

1 tsp ground cumin

¼ tsp ground cloves

½ tsp ground ginger

½ tsp ground cardamom

½ tsp ground coriander

½ tsp allspice

4 spring onions, trimmed and sliced

1 red chilli, deseeded and finely chopped

Juice of 5 oranges, plus the zest of 1

400g tin chickpeas

60g sultanas

250ml vegetable stock

240g couscous

3 tbsp fresh mint, chopped

20g pinenuts

Salt and white pepper

Barbecued pepper melts (v)

Perfect on a summer BBQ, these tasty morsels make the most of elongated Romano peppers, which are sweeter than the everyday capsicums. They look great on a platter and make for easy-to-eat party food.

Serves 6
Ready in 30 minutes

1 Heat the barbecue or preheat the grill and slice 2 of the pepper halves. Heat the oil in a large pan, add the onions and sliced peppers and cook, stirring, for 5–8 minutes, until softened and golden. Stir in the balsamic vinegar.

2 Place the pepper halves on a plate (to transfer to the barbecue later) or place on a grill pan if grilling, and then spoon the onion mixture into the pepper halves. Top each with a sprig of thyme and then a slice of cheese. Season with pepper.

3 Barbecue for 15–20 minutes or 10–15 minutes under the grill, until the peppers are tender and the cheese has melted. Serve.

4 various colour Romano peppers, halved lengthways
2 tbsp olive oil
2 onions, thinly sliced
1 tbsp balsamic vinegar
6 fresh sprigs of thyme
120g Taleggio or another tangy cheese, thinly sliced
Black pepper

Contributed by Waitrose Fresh Produce

Hot guacamole (V)

Perfect as a snack or party food with red or yellow pepper crudités, Facing Heaven Chilli Company's guacamole takes advantage of one of the hottest chillies around, the Scotch bonnet (see page 16 for details). This is red hot and not for the faint hearted.

Serves 4-6
Ready in 15 minutes, plus chilling time

1 Cut each avocado in half, remove the stone and scoop the flesh into a food processor using a dessert spoon. Add the garlic, lime juice, salt, sugar and chilli and pulse until nearly smooth. Transfer to a serving bowl and chill until needed.

2 To blanch the tomatoes, remove the cores with a knife and cut a crisscross into each one on at the bottom and place them in a large bowl of boiling water, standing for 2 minutes. Drain and refresh with cold water. You should be able to peel the skin easily, then deseed by cutting in half and hollowing out the seeds with a teaspoon. Chop the flesh into pieces.

3 Mix the tomato flesh into the chilled avocado mixture and drizzle with olive oil. Season with black pepper and chill for at least 20 minutes or until needed. Serve alongside the pepper crudités.

4 ripe Hass avocados

3 cloves of garlic

Juice of 1½ limes

2 tsp sea salt

½ tsp sugar

1 red Scotch bonnet chilli, chopped (or 2 tsp Facing Heaven Habanero Chilli Sauce)

2 beef tomatoes

1 tbsp olive oil

4 red and yellow bell peppers, deseeded and cut into sticks/crudités

Black pepper

By the Facing Heaven Chilli Company

Berry and red pepper smoothie (v)

Packed full of vitamin C, this unusual combination for a smoothie is a real flavour revelation. And with a healthy shot of oats, it's a swift breakfast on the go. Remember, peppers are fruit too!

Serves 4
Ready in 5 minutes

1 In a food processor, with a handheld blender in a bowl or in a smoothie maker, combine the apples, banana, pepper, raspberries and/or strawberries, honey (if using) and oats. Blend for 30 seconds, or until completely puréed, and slowly blend in the apple juice.

2 Add the ice and blend for 15 seconds. Divide into four glass tumblers or chill in a sealed container and keep for up to three days.

2 red apples, peeled, cored and chopped

1 banana, chopped

1 red bell pepper, deseeded and chopped

200g fresh or frozen raspberries and/or strawberries

1 tsp honey (optional)

25g oats

1 litre apple juice

Tip

If you fancy a creamier breakfast smoothie replace the apple juice with a combination of 500ml skimmed milk and 500ml natural yogurt.

Chilli hot chocolate (v)

Fast becoming an everyday pairing, chilli and chocolate works, especially with a good-quality dark chocolate. You don't have to use 70% cocoa chocolate if you don't have it, but it really does make a difference to your tastebuds! This is a thick and creamy hot chocolate and can act as a simple dessert at a wintery dinner party.

Serves 4-6
Ready in 25 minutes

1 In a large saucepan, simmer the milk for 1–2 minutes, until just warm. Off the heat, add the chilli and stand to infuse for 15 minutes.

2 Return the saucepan to a low heat and pour in the single cream and add the chocolate. Stir until all the chocolate has melted. Discard the chilli. Divide between mugs or glasses, and swirl a teaspoon of single cream in a swirl into each. Serve with shortbread to dip in.

1 litre whole fat milk
1 red bird's eye chilli, pricked
200ml single cream, plus extra to decorate
200g 70% dark chocolate, chopped
Shortbread fingers, to serve

By Liz O'Keefe

Spicy tofu and noodle soup (v)

Tasty any time of the year, this Chinese-style soup is warming and refreshing – and a meal in itself. The fruit is an everyday staple in China, where the most peppers are grown.

Serves 4
Ready in 40 minutes

1 Heat 1 tbsp of the oil in a large saucepan over a medium heat and add the shallots and garlic. Cook, stirring, for 1 minute, then stir in the ginger, peppers, chillies and mushrooms. Cook, stirring, for 4-5 minutes, until softened.

2 Pour in the stock and bring to the boil. Add the lemongrass and simmer for 10 minutes.

3 Meanwhile, on a plate, combine the flour with the five spice and then coat the tofu in it, using a teaspoon, so the tofu doesn't break up. Heat the remaining oil in a frying pan and then fry the tofu cubes for 1 minute, then turn over once and fry for 1-2 minutes, until golden. Drain on kitchen paper.

4 Add the noodles, spring onions and lime juice and simmer for a further 3-4 minutes, until the noodles are tender. Divide between four bowls and top with pieces of the tofu and season with the sesame oil and soy sauce, before serving.

3 tbsp vegetable oil

2 shallots, chopped

1 clove of garlic, finely sliced

1cm piece fresh root ginger, finely chopped

3 various colour bell peppers, deseeded and chopped

2 red chillies, deseeded and finely chopped

200g mixed exotic mushrooms, roughly sliced

1 litre vegetable stock

1 stem lemongrass, bruised

3 tbsp cornflour

1 tsp Chinese five spice

300g tofu, drained and cut into slabs

2 spring onions, trimmed and finely chopped

Juice of ½ lime

600g rice noodles

2 tbsp sesame oil

2 tbsp soy sauce

By Liz O'Keefe

Steamed Vietnamese stuffed peppers

Here our beloved stuffed peppers have been given a Vietnamese edge, combining the winning team of peppers, beef and black beans in a traditional Southeast Asian dish.

Serves 4
Ready in 50 minutes

1 Heat the sunflower oil in a frying pan and add the peppers. Fry until slightly brown, turning regularly. Drain on kitchen paper. In a large mixing bowl, combine the minced beef, salt and crushed stock cube and fill the pepper halves with the mixture.

2 Return the frying pan to the heat and add the black beans, white wine, spring onions and honey, along with a tablespoon of cold water and cook for 1-2 minutes, until reduced and thick.

3 Place the peppers in a metal or wicker steamer and place on top of a pan to boil. Divide the black bean mixture between each halved peppers and cover with the steamer lid. Steam for 35-40 minutes, until the mince is cooked thoroughly. Serve two pepper halves each, with rice noodles.

2 tbsp sunflower oil

4 various colour bell peppers, stalks trimmed, cut in half horizontally and deseeded

500g minced beef

1 tsp salt

¼ chicken stock cube, crushed

50g fermented black beans

50ml white wine

4 spring onions, trimmed and chopped

½ tsp honey

Rice noodles, to serve

By Kim Nyugen

Chorizo, yellow pepper and basil penne

This simple Spanish-style supper makes the most of the sweetest bell pepper of them all, which hardly needs any cooking.

Serves 4
Ready in 15 minutes

1 Heat two-thirds of the olive oil in a large frying pan and sauté the garlic and red onion for 2–3 minutes, until they begin to soften. Add the chorizo and cook for a further 5 minutes. Mix in the peppers and lemon juice, and cook on low for 5 minutes.

2 Meanwhile, in a saucepan, cover the penne in boiling water and cook for 5 minutes. Drain.

3 Stir the remaining olive oil and half the basil into the drained penne. Season and stir in the chorizo mixture, along with the Parmesan and remaining basil. Serve immediately.

3 tbsp extra virgin olive oil
1 clove of garlic, crushed
2 red onions, roughly chopped
225g Spanish chorizo, thickly sliced
3 yellow bell peppers, deseeded and roughly chopped
Juice of 1 lemon
300g fresh penne
7g fresh basil, roughly chopped
50g Parmesan shavings
Salt and black pepper

By Dr Neal Ward of pepper grower Cantelo Nurseries

Virgin pepper Mary (V)

Serving as both a great hangover cure and cold remedy, not to mention a mean Bloody Mary with a shot of vodka or a splash of gin, this drink is the best way to get that much-needed vitamin shot.

Serves 2
Ready in 5 minutes

1 In a food processor or liquidizer, combine the tomatoes, cucumber, peppers, ginger and lemon. Blend until very smooth. This will probably take 2–3 minutes. Mix in the cayenne pepper and season with salt and pepper.

2 Divide the mixture between two glasses filled with ice and decorate with a few celery sticks and a grinding of black pepper.

Tip

 This is a great start to a dinner party, served in shot or sherry glasses as an aperitif.

3 Elegance tomatoes, cored

½ cucumber, peeled

2 mini sweet peppers or 1 red bell pepper, deseeded and chopped

0.5cm piece of fresh root ginger, grated

Half a lemon, peeled and pips removed

Pinch of cayenne pepper

½ stick of celery, cut into fine sticks

Salt and black pepper

Ice, to serve

By pepper grower Thanet Earth chef
Jason Freedman

Salsa salu (v)

This traditional Uruguayan vegetable sauce makes a hero out of peppers and is usually served with steak or cold meats, as well as at barbeques. Make it to serve with dinner, or cook up a batch and store in jars in the fridge and use as a sauce for the rest of the week.

Makes approx. 1 litre
Ready in 1 hour 10 minutes

1 To blanch the tomatoes, remove the cores with a knife and cut a crisscross into each one on at the bottom. Place in a bowl and cover with boiling water for 2 minutes. Drain and refresh until cold in running cold water. The skins of the tomatoes should peel away easily. Discard the skins and remove the seeds.

2 In a food processor, blend the tomato flesh, onions, garlic, red pepper, chilli, carrot and olives with a third of the oil. Heat the remaining oil in a large saucepan and add the blended mixture. Cook, stirring, for 2 minutes, then pour in the white wine and stock, and bring to the boil.

3 Stir well and add the paprika, bay leaf and rosemary. Simmer for 45–50 minutes until thick and glossy. Remove the bay leave and rosemary before serving or storing.

3 beef tomatoes
2 onions, finely chopped
2 cloves of garlic, crushed
4 red bell peppers, deseeded and chopped
1 red chilli pepper, deseeded and chopped
1 carrot, grated
2 tbsp pitted black and green olives, chopped
2 tsp paprika
50ml olive oil
80ml white wine
250ml stock
1 bay leaf
1 sprig of rosemary

Goat's cheese, walnut and chicory salad with yellow pepper dressing (v)

Great with bread for a lunch, as a side dish or as part of a tapas feast, this bitter, sweet and creamy salad highlights the sweetness of yellow peppers.

Serves 2-4
Ready in 10 minutes

1 In food processor or in a bowl with a hand-held blender, blend the pepper, Prosecco jelly or honey, oil and vinegar together, then season with salt and pepper.

2 In a large serving dish, arrange the chicory leaves, walnuts and goat's cheese and then dress with the mixture made in step 1. Serve.

1 yellow bell pepper, deseeded and chopped

1 tbsp Prosecco jelly or honey

3 tbsp rapeseed oil

1 tbsp white wine vinegar

2 x 150g rinded goat's cheese, broken into small pieces

1 tbsp walnuts, roughly chopped

2 white chicory heads, trimmed

Sea salt and black pepper

By Liz O'Keefe

Gazpacho (v)

Great for the summer months, Dutch chef Guus Vredenburg's gazpacho recipe is quick and tasty. Traditionally a Mediterranean dish, this thick soup is served chilled and is full of vitamins, as all of the vegetables used are eaten raw.

Serves 6
Ready in 10 minutes, plus chilling

1 Place the tomatoes in a food processor and blitz until a purée. Sieve the purée into a bowl and discard the seeds and skin. Return the sieved purée to the food processor and add the cucumber, red onion, red and green peppers, chilli and garlic and whizz until smooth.

2 Stir in the olive oil and sherry vinegar and 3 tbsp cold water while the motor is running. The consistency of the soup should now be creamy. Season with salt to taste, then chill for 5 minutes or until you serve.

Tip

 Make this soup a meal by garnishing with smoked ricotta or adding chopped tiger prawns and dill.

1kg on-the-vine tomatoes, chopped

1 cucumber, peeled, deseeded and chopped

1 red onion, chopped

4 red and green bell peppers, deseeded and chopped

1 green chilli, deseeded and finely chopped

1 clove of garlic, chopped

1 tbsp extra virgin olive oil

60ml sherry vinegar or dry sherry

Sea salt

By Guus Vredenburg on behalf of the Colourful Taste pepper campaign

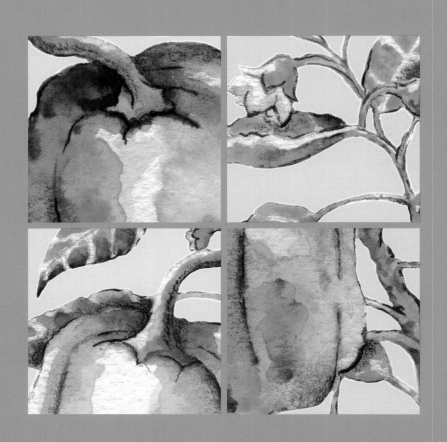

Recipes with a Little Extra Effort

Mixed pickled peppers (v)

Would you too like to pick a peck of pickled peppers? Well, now you can with a recipe that combines every and any pepper you can find. Pickled peppers are great with tapas, cold meats and barbecues – any time or place.

Makes 3 litres
Ready in 20 minutes, plus storing

1 Cut two small slits in each of the peppers and chillies you are using whole. Tightly pack 1 clove of garlic, 1 bay leaf and 1 chilli and a variety of peppers into the hot sterilized jars (see the tip below), scattering the capers and peppercorns throughout and leaving a 1cm gap at the top.

2 In a large saucepan, combine the vinegar, 200ml of cold water, salt and sugar. Bring to boil and then simmer for 5 minutes. Pour the liquid into the jars, leaving a little room at the top and put the lids on. Label with the date and "Ready to eat in six weeks".

Tip

To sterilize the jars, wash the jars and lids in soapy water and rinse completely. Place in an oven preheated at 140C/gas 1 and turn the oven off once the door is shut. Remove in 20 minutes and fill immediately.

3kg various colour mini, long and bell peppers, sliced and whole

3 red chillies, whole (optional)

3 cloves of garlic, unpeeled

3 bay leaves

2 tsp capers

20 whole peppercorns and pink peppercorns

600ml white wine vinegar

1 tbsp salt

8-10 tbsp sugar

By Liz O'Keefe

Red pepper, feta and mint muffins (v)

Great to make together, these tasty nutrient-packed muffins will be loved by both children and adults, as a quick snack or lunch. They are also very handy for lunchboxes.

Makes 12
Ready in 45 minutes

1 Preheat the oven 190C/gas 5 and line two six-hole muffin trays with greaseproof muffin cases or fashion them out of baking paper (see tip). In a large mixing bowl, combine the flour, baking powder and salt and in a separate jug, mix together the oil, honey, eggs and milk. Pour the oil mixture gradually into the dry ingredients, stirring as you go, until just combined.

2 Season the mixture with pepper and gently fold in the peppers, feta and mint, then divide the batter between the muffin cases. Bake for 30–35 minutes, until a flat knife comes out clean when inserted. Serve hot with butter or store in a cake tin.

190g plain flour, sifted

2 tsp baking powder

Pinch of salt

60ml rapeseed oil

1 tbsp honey

1 medium egg

180ml milk

3 red bell peppers, deseeded and finely chopped

100g feta, chopped into small cubes

14g fresh mint, torn

Black pepper

Tip

To make your own muffin cases, cut a sheet of baking paper into squares and make two or three folds in the squares so they fit the muffin tray.

By Liz O'Keefe

Brazilian black bean soup

A traditional Brazilian dish, this soup can either be a filling meal or a delicate starter by changing the portion size. We've added an orange pepper purée to bring the recipe to life – mix it in as you eat, along with the sliced raw onion, coriander and sour cream, to coax the rich black bean flavours out.

Serves 4-6
Ready in 1 hour

1 In a large saucepan, heat 3 tsp of the olive oil and sauté the onions and garlic for 8-10 minutes, until very soft. Add the sugar, two-thirds of the peppers, carrot, cumin and paprika and cook for 5 minutes.

2 Mix in the black beans and cook for 1 minute, then pour in the chicken stock. Simmer, stirring occasionally for 30 minutes. Stir in the orange juice and season with black pepper. Simmer for a further 10 minutes, until thick and condensed.

3 Meanwhile, in a food processor or with a hand-held blender, purée the remaining chopped peppers with the orange zest and remaining teaspoon of oil and season with salt.

4 In the processor or with the blender, liquidize the soup (you may have to do this in batches, depending on the size of your processor). Chill for 2 hours if you would like to eat cold or serve straight away, garnished with the sour cream, puréed pepper and coriander, and serve with extra coriander and sliced onions.

Tip

This soup is great chilled in the summer and warm in the winter as a coarser soup. For a coarser soup, just leave out the liquidizing in step 4 and make sure all the chopped ingredients are chopped finely before you start cooking.

4 tsp olive oil
3 onions, chopped
2 cloves of garlic, crushed
Pinch of sugar
4 orange bell peppers, deseeded and chopped
1 carrot, finely chopped
1 tsp cumin
1 tsp paprika
2 x 400g tins black beans
250ml chicken or vegetable stock
200ml orange juice
Zest of 1 orange
Salt and black pepper
Sour cream, sliced onions and fresh coriander, to serve

By Liz O'Keefe

Pepper balti (v)

A British favourite, this Pakistani curry makes mini sweet peppers the star. You can add anything to a balti — just start with the curry paste in step 1 and add whatever vegetables and meat you'd like, followed by tomatoes and water.

Serves 4
Ready in 30 minutes

1 In a small blender, combine the shallots, tomato purée, chilli powder, garam masala, cumin seeds, garlic, ginger, chilli and its seeds, salt and vegetable oil, to make a paste. Heat a wok or large frying pan and add the paste. Fry, stirring, for 1 minute, until the air is fragrant.

2 Add the peppers and the lemon juice and fry for 2 minutes, before adding the tomatoes and 100ml water. Bring to the boil, then simmer, covered, for 15 minutes, or until the peppers are softened, adding more water if the sauce becomes too dry.

3 Mix in the spinach and coriander, then cover and cook for 2 minutes to wilt the leaves. Stir in the yogurt and serve with rice, popadoms, chutneys and raita.

Tips

To make a cooling raita, grate ½ cucumber into a bowl and season with salt. Mix in 75ml natural yogurt, zest and juice of ½ lemon and 2 tbsp chopped fresh mint leaves and season with black pepper.

For a milder balti, deseed the chilli and only add the flesh. If you do not enjoy heat at all, remove the fresh chilli from the recipe completely.

2 shallots, chopped

3 tbsp tomato purée

1 tsp chilli powder

1 tsp garam masala

½ tsp cumin seeds, crushed

1 clove of garlic, crushed

1cm piece of fresh root ginger, grated

1 red bird's eye chilli, chopped

Pinch of salt

4 tbsp vegetable oil

500g mini sweet peppers, cored at the top (see prep on page 22) and deseeded

Juice of ½ lemon

400g tin chopped tomatoes

400g baby spinach leaves

7g fresh coriander, chopped

2 tbsp Greek yogurt

Steamed rice, popadoms, chutneys and raita (see tip), to serve

By Liz O'Keefe

Orange pepper cheesecake

Sweet orange bell peppers are the perfect partner for cream cheese, whether they are stuffed with it or paired in a sandwich, so why not join them in a cheesecake? The proof is in the pudding…

Serves 8-10
Ready in 20 minutes, plus chilling time

1 Grease a 23cm round loose-bottomed cake tin with the extra butter. In a small saucepan or in a bowl in the microwave, gently melt the butter until a liquid. In a large bowl, crush the digestive biscuits with the end of a rolling pin, then stir in the melted butter to combine. Fill the greased tin with the mixture and press down with the back of a metal dessert spoon to form an even biscuit base. Chill for an hour.

2 Meanwhile, in a food processor or with a hand-held blender, purée the peppers. In a separate large bowl, cream the cheese and icing sugar together with the back of a wooden spoon. Mix in the pepper purée and cream, and whisk for 2 minutes until thick. Pour onto the biscuit base and level with the back of a clean dessertspoon. Chill overnight or for at least 3 hours.

3 To serve, loosen the cheesecake from the tin by running a knife dipped in hot water around the sides, then ease the bottom of the tin up from the underside of the tin. Place on a serving plate and dust with icing sugar before serving.

Tip

When using a loose-bottomed tin to make cheesecake, it can be hard to remove the biscuit base. Avoid this by covering the bottom with cling film, twisting it together on the other side to keep in place. After you remove the sides, just lift either side of the cling film to transfer the cheesecake to a serving dish.

75g butter, melted, plus extra to grease

150g digestive biscuits

2 orange bell peppers, skinned and puréed

400g cream cheese

150g icing sugar, plus extra to dust

300ml thick double cream, whipped

By pepper grower Tangmere Airfield Nurseries

Red pepper and cream cheese cupcakes

Who said carrots could be the only veg to grace a cake? Red peppers are perfect in a cake batter – and make for an interesting and totally natural colour too!

Makes 12
Ready in 45 minutes, plus cooling time

1 Preheat the oven to 180C/gas 4 and line two six-hole cupcake trays with cases. In a large bowl, cream the butter and sugar together with the back of a wooden spoon until light and fluffy. Beat in the eggs one at a time, then mix in the red peppers.

2 Add the baking powder and then a spoonful of the flour, folding it into the mixture gently. Repeat until the remaining flour has been fully incorporated. Stir in the milk and vanilla. Pour the batter into the cupcake cases and bake for 20-25 minutes, until a flat knife comes out clean when inserted. Place on a wire rack to cool.

3 Once the cakes have cooled, place the cream cheese in a bowl and cream the icing sugar into it. Add the lemon juice and stir. Use a spatula to ice each cake with the cream cheese icing and sprinkle with the reserved grated pepper.

200g butter, softened
200g caster sugar
2 eggs
4 red bell peppers, deseeded and grated, reserving a little for decoration
250g self-raising flour, sifted
1 tsp baking powder
1 tbsp milk
1 tsp vanilla bean extract
100g cream cheese
200g icing sugar
2 tsp lemon juice

By Liz O'Keefe

Roast tomato and red pepper relish (v)

This simple chutney makes a great accompaniment for any curry, cheese or cold meats. Keep chilled for up to a week for a handy and tasty relish.

Makes approx. 350g
Ready in 20 minutes, plus cooling time

1 Preheat the oven to 220C/gas 7. Place the tomatoes and peppers, skin-side up, on a baking tray, then drizzle with half the olive oil and sprinkle with salt. Roast for 10-15 minutes, until the skins blister.

2 Place the tomatoes and peppers in a bowl, cover with cling film and allow to cool. Once cooled, peel the skin off the tomatoes and peppers and discard. Transfer the tomato and pepper flesh into a food processor and add the garlic, sugar, coconut and remaining oil. Blend the ingredients until smooth, then store or serve.

Tips

Try this relish alongside the Pepper balti on page 56 and see page 50 for tips on how to sterilize jars before storing the relish.

3 beef tomatoes, cored and quartered

2 red bell peppers, halved

3 tbsp olive oil

1 clove of garlic, chopped

1 tsp sugar

2 tbsp desiccated coconut

Sea salt

Hearty meatballs

Proving meatballs aren't just about the meat, these bundles of taste from the British Heart Foundation are a combination of mince and textured veg, making a meatball that's great for your heart. This dish contains 558 calories, 16g fat, 1.3g salt and 21.6g sugar.

Serves 2
Ready in 35 minutes, plus chilling time

1 In a large bowl, combine the beef, half the shallots, the courgette, breadcrumbs, 1 tbsp of the tomato purée, the garlic and the oregano and/or thyme. Dust your hands with the flour and shape mixture into eight even balls. Place them on a plate and chill for 20 minutes.

2 Preheat the oven to 180C/gas 4, then heat the oil in a non-stick frying pan. Fry the chilled meatballs for 6-7 minutes or until sealed completely. Transfer meatballs to an ovenproof dish and cover with tin foil.

3 In the same frying pan, sauté the remaining shallots and pepper for 1 minute, then add the remaining tomato purée, tomatoes and carrot. Cook stirring for a further 1 minute, then mix in the ketchup and stock. Bring gently to the boil, stirring occasionally. Pour sauce over meatballs, cover again with the foil and bake for 10-15 minutes, until the meatballs are cooked through and the sauce is thick. Serve with pasta, bread or more vegetables and garnish with basil.

55g extra lean minced beef
4 shallots, finely chopped
1 courgette, grated
25g fresh breadcrumbs (see tip)
2 tbsp tomato purée
1 clove of garlic, crushed
7g fresh basil and/or oregano, chopped
1 tbsp plain flour
2 tsp sunflower oil
1 red bell pepper, deseeded and chopped
227g tin chopped tomatoes
1 carrot, grated
125ml vegetable stock
1 tbsp tomato ketchup
Black pepper
Pasta or bread, to serve

Tip

To make your own breadcrumbs, save up some older ends of bread (you can freeze them as they accumulate, in advance) and whizz them up in a food processor until fine.

By the British Heart Foundation

Pepper, aubergine and goat's cheese tart (v)

Peppers aren't just mighty tasty, they can add some fabulous colour to traditional dishes, too. Here, English pepper grower Abbey View Produce shares its Pepper, aubergine and goat's cheese tart, complete with red pepper in the pastry.

Serves 6-8
Ready in 1 hour 25 minutes, plus chilling time

1 To make the red pepper shortcrust pastry, in a food processor, purée 1 of the red peppers until a fine paste. In a large mixing bowl, combine the flour, lemon zest and salt, then mix in the red pepper purée. Add the butter cubes and rub in the butter with your fingertips until the mixture resembles fine breadcrumbs and the butter is fully combined with the flour.

2 Gradually add 1 tsp to 1 tbsp of cold water to the dry mixture, mixing with a knife and then your hands, until it forms a firm pastry ball. If it's too dry, add a little more cold water. If it's too moist, add a little more flour. Wrap the pastry ball in cling film and chill for 30 minutes.

3 Preheat the oven to 200C/gas 6 and grease a tart tin. On a clean surface, dusted with flour, roll out the pastry to fit the tin. Line the tin with the pastry, cutting away any excess and cover with baking paper and baking beans. Bake blind for 10-15 minutes, until golden. Remove the paper and beans, then turn the oven to 180C/gas 4.

4 Meanwhile, heat the olive oil in a frying pan and sauté the onion for 2–3 minutes, until softened. Add the onion, aubergine, garlic and remaining pepper, and cook, stirring, on a low heat for 8–10 minutes, until the aubergines are soft. Season and allow to cool .

5 In a large bowl, whisk the eggs and milk together and add 150g of the goat's cheese, as well as the thyme and cooled onion, aubergine and pepper mix. Pour the entire mixture into the pastry case then crumble the remaining goat's cheese on top. Season with pepper. Bake for 40-45 minutes, until the filling is set, then serve, garnished with thyme and black pepper.

2 red bell peppers, deseeded and sliced

250g plain flour, sifted, plus extra for dusting

Zest of 1 lemon

Pinch of salt

110g chilled unsalted butter, chopped, plus extra for greasing

2 tbsp olive oil

1 red onion, sliced

1 aubergine, sliced

1 clove of garlic, crushed

2 eggs

180ml milk

200g soft goat's cheese, crumbled

7g fresh thyme leaves, plus extra for garnish

Black pepper

You will also need:
Baking paper
Baking beans

Tip

Your hands and utensils have to be very cold to make pastry, so it is light and fluffy when it is cooked. Some people freeze and then grate the butter and others use iced water instead of cold or chill their rolling pin, if their hands are naturally hotter than most.

By pepper grower Abbey View Produce

Jambalaya

Inspired by Spanish paella, the jambalaya was created in the US and has a sausage, prawn, pepper and rice base. We've added some sweet, long, pointed peppers to ours, as well as one of the hottest chillies – the Scotch bonnet.

Serves 4-6
Ready in 1 hour 25 minutes

1 Combine the cornflour and Cajun spice in either a freezer bag or bowl, then add the chicken thighs and coat them completely. In a very large ovenproof pan or dish, heat the olive oil until sizzling, then add the chicken, skin down. Cook for 1-2 minutes, until golden, then turn and cook for the same amount, until the thighs are sealed.

2 Turn the heat down and add the celery, onions and garlic. Sauté for 2-3 minutes, then add the chilli, peppers and smoked sausage. Cook, stirring, for 2 minutes then add the white wine, simmering for another 2 minutes. Stir in the tomatoes and stock, and bring to the boil. Add the rice, stir and cover, simmering for 35-40 minutes, until the rice is fluffy and the sauce is on the dry side.

3 Preheat the oven to 190C/gas 5. Stir in the prawns and/or squid, season with salt and pepper and mix in the parsley. Bake, covered, for 5 minutes, making sure that the prawns and/or squid are cooked thoroughly before serving with lemon wedges.

2 tbsp cornflour
1 tbsp Cajun spice
4 chicken thighs, skin on
4 tbsp olive oil
4 celery sticks, chopped
2 onions, chopped
1 clove of garlic, thinly sliced
1 Scotch bonnet chilli, deseeded and chopped
4 various colour pointed peppers, thickly sliced
100g smoked sausage, thickly sliced
100ml white wine
400g tin chopped tomatoes
500ml chicken stock
500g long grain rice
250g raw king prawns and/or chopped squid
7g fresh flat leaf parsley, chopped
Salt and black pepper
Lemon wedges, to serve

Madagascar chicken

Originating in Africa, Madagascar chicken uses yellow bell peppers to make a particularly colourful mild curry. Here, we portion a chicken to make the most of all those flavours and a thriftier meal.

Serves 4-6
Ready in 40 minutes, plus marinating time

1 In a plastic bowl, season the chicken pieces with salt and pepper and then marinate in the lemon juice for 30 minutes. Heat half of the olive oil in a frying pan and add the chicken. Fry until sealed, then set aside.

2 In the same pan, add the remaining oil and fry the onions and garlic for 2-3 minutes, until softened. Stir in the yellow peppers and cook for 5 minutes. Add the coconut milk, ground ginger, cayenne pepper, lemon zest and 200ml water. Return the chicken to the pan, cover and simmer for 20–25 minutes, until reduced and the chicken is completely cooked through. Serve with steamed white rice.

1 chicken, quartered, or 2 chicken thighs, 2 wings and 2 breasts (see tip)

Zest and juice of 2 lemons

2 tbsp olive oil

2 onions, chopped

2 cloves of garlic, crushed

4 yellow bell peppers, deseeded and chopped

400ml coconut milk

2 tsp ground ginger

Pinch of cayenne pepper

Salt and black pepper

Steamed rice, to serve

Tip

To quarter your own chicken, place the chicken in front of you, legs first. Holding one leg, push it down to the board, breaking the bone joint, then make an incision at a 45° angle, cutting across the skin and through to cut the leg off. Repeat with the other leg at a 315° angle. Turn the chicken around so the wings are facing you and break the bone joint at the base of the wing and cut the wing off. Repeat with the other wing. Next, cut two lines towards you, either side of the middle of the ribcage in the middle of bird, then cut through that line, keeping the knife flat against the ribcage to remove all of the breast in one piece. Do the same with the other side. Use the carcass to make chicken stock.

Make chicken stock

Use the chicken carcass to make a rich, homemade chicken stock. Place the carcass in a large saucepan and add 2 tbsp whole peppercorns, 1 bay leaf, a bouquet of herbs (sprigs of mint, parsley, rosemary and thyme, tied together with kitchen string) and a pinch of sea salt. Cover with boiling water, then bring to the boil. Simmer, covered, for 20 minutes. Sieve and discard the carcass, making sure you scrape all the meat off, then pour the liquid into a jug. Freeze portions in freezer bags if not being used straight away.

Chilli and red pepper chocolate mousse

Now we are all used to the chilli and chocolate combo, it's time to throw chilli's big sister the bell pepper into the mix. Here, that delicate red pepper taste brings a sweet addition to the dark chocolate's sour. Combined with the heat of the chilli and the coolness of the mousse, this really does cause a sense sensation.

Serves 4
Ready in 20 minutes, plus chilling time

1 In a bowl with a hand–held blender, purée the pepper and chilli until a very smooth paste. Add the egg yolks and combine.

2 In a microwave, melt the chocolate in a plastic bowl for 30 second blasts at a time, until the chocolate squares are just losing their shape and on melting point. Stir the chocolate and then mix it into the egg mixture and combine thoroughly.

3 In a separate large bowl, whisk the egg whites for 3-4 minutes, until stiff peaks, then gently fold in the chocolate mixture. Divide between four serving glasses or ramekins and chill overnight, or for at least 2 hours until firm.

4 To serve, whisk the double cream in a small bowl until just thick and top each mousse with a dollop. Decorate with the grated extra chocolate and serve.

1 red bell pepper, deseeded and chopped

1 red chilli, deseeded and chopped

4 eggs, separated

200g 70% dark chocolate, chopped, plus extra for grating

50ml double cream

By Liz O'Keefe

African sunrise salad (v)

A South African dish, this healthy, nutty vegan salad combines refreshing ingredients perfect for a summer's day.

Serves 4
Ready in 45 minutes

1 In a saucepan, cover the pearl barley with cold water, then bring to the boil. Simmer for 30–35 minutes or until al dente. Drain and refresh with cold water.

2 Meanwhile, dry-fry the linseed, pumpkin seeds, sunflower seeds, sesame seeds and pinenuts in a non-stick frying pan for 1–2 minutes, then set aside. For the dressing, combine the olive oil, balsamic vinegar and honey in a small bowl or jug. Season.

3 Mix the pearl barley and the toasted seeds and nuts together with the peppers, cucumber, tomato, curry powder and paprika in a large salad bowl, then mix through the dressing. Rest for 5 minutes, then mix in the parsley and serve.

150g pearl barley

1 tbsp each of linseed, pumpkin seeds, sunflower seeds and sesame seeds

1 tbsp pinenuts

3 tbsp olive oil

2 tbsp balsamic vinegar

1 tbsp honey

3 red, yellow and orange bell peppers, deseeded and diced

½ cucumber, diced

1 tomato, cored and diced

Pinch each of medium curry powder and smoked paprika

7g fresh curly parsley, finely chopped

Salt and black pepper

Puppy breath chilli

For all the chilli enthusiasts out there, Facing Heaven Chilli Company's Puppy breath chilli will bring a tear to your eye. And with a whole head of garlic thrown into the mix, remember to enjoy this with caution!

Serves 4-6
Ready in 1 hour 40 minutes

1 In small batches if necessary and using a large saucepan, brown and seal the steak in the groundnut oil. Add the onion, peppers and garlic and fry for 2 minutes, before stirring in the tomatoes.

2 Add the chilli paste or chillies, celery, Worcestershire sauce, cumin and paprika and bring to the boil. Simmer, stirring occasionally, for 1 hour and 30 minutes, or until the meat is tender. Off the heat, stir in the blackstrap molasses or black treacle and a pinch of salt, then serve with rice.

2 tbsp groundnut oil

1kg chopped stewing steak

2 onions, chopped

6 green and red bell peppers, deseeded and chopped

1 head of garlic, chopped

2 x 400g tin chopped tomatoes

75g Facing Heaven Bowl O'Soul Chilli Paste or 2 Scotch bonnet chillies, chopped

2 celery sticks, chopped

2 tsp Worcestershire sauce

3 tsp ground cumin

3 tsp ground paprika

1 tbsp blackstrap molasses or black treacle

Salt

Steamed rice, to serve

By the Facing Heaven Chilli Company

Peperonata (v)

This rich Italian family favourite can be served either hot with steak and pasta or cold as an accompaniment for all manner of pies, meats and cheeses. You'll never go back to ketchup again.

Makes 1.5 litres
Ready in 1 hour 10 minutes

1 Preheat the oven to 190C/gas 5. Place the peppers on baking trays and roast, turning regularly for 15–20 minutes, or until the skins begin to blacken. Place in a bowl, cover with cling film and leave to cool. Once cool, remove and discard the skins, then deseed the peppers, retaining the juices in a small bowl. Tear the flesh of the peppers into strips.

2 Meanwhile, in a saucepan, heat the oil and sauté the garlic for 2 minutes. Stir in the tomato purée, then mix in the diced tomatoes gradually, as well as the sugar and vinegar. Sauté for 5–10 minutes, then add the tomato juice and the juices from the peppers. Simmer for 15–20 minutes, stirring occasionally.

3 Mix in the pepper strips, olives and capers. Add the salt and pepper. Simmer, covered but stirring occasionally, for 25–30 minutes. Add the basil and rest for 5 minutes before serving with hot steak or bottling (see page 50 for storage and sterilization tips). Store chilled for up to a week.

16 various colour bell peppers
2 tbsp olive oil
6 cloves of garlic, crushed
75g tomato purée
6 beef tomatoes, cored and diced
2 tbsp sugar
50ml red wine vinegar
750ml tomato juice
400g pitted Kalamata black olives in oil, drained and chopped
2 tbsp capers, chopped
4g fresh basil leaves, roughly torn
Sea salt and black pepper

By Attilio Duranti

Thai green crab curry

Once you've mastered a Thai curry paste, you can curry anything, so if you don't fancy crabmeat, just replace with any fish or meat. Green peppers are especially suited to this dish, complementing the fresh green flavours of the lemongrass, limes and sugarsnap peas.

Serves 2
Ready in 25 minutes

1 In a small blender, combine the shallots, garlic, ginger, coriander stalks, chilli and its seeds, lime zest, fish sauce, sesame and vegetable oil and sugar to make a paste. Heat a wok or large frying pan and add the paste. Fry, stirring, for 1 minute, until the air is fragrant.

2 Add the green peppers and stir-fry for 2 minutes, then stir in the dark crabmeat/dressed crab. Squeeze in half of the lime juice, followed by the coconut milk and 200ml water. Stir thoroughly and add the lime leaves and lemongrass. Bring to the boil and simmer for 10 minutes, until reduced by half.

3 Add the peas/mangetout and sweetcorn and cook for 3 minutes, then stir in the white crabmeat and the coriander leaves. Cook, covered, for 2 minutes, making sure the crabmeat is piping hot. Serve, garnished with coriander and with steamed rice, along with soy sauce to taste.

Tip

If you don't fancy your curry hot, just discard the chilli seeds instead of adding them into the mix.

2 shallots, chopped

1 clove of garlic, chopped

1cm piece Thai ginger (galangal), chopped

7g fresh coriander leaves and stalks, plus extra leaves for garnish

2 green bird's eye chillies (see tip)

Zest and juice of 1 lime

1 tbsp Thai fish sauce

2 tsp sesame oil

2 tsp vegetable oil

2 tsp palm or brown sugar

2 green bell peppers, deseeded and thinly sliced

2 prepared crabs or 1 tin of dressed crab and 2 tins of white crabmeat

400ml tin of coconut milk

4 kaffir lime leaves

1 stem lemongrass, bruised

200g sugarsnap peas or mangetout and baby sweetcorn, halved lengthways

Steamed rice and soy sauce, to serve

By Liz O'Keefe

Chicken and pepper risotto

Make this creamy rice-based Italian classic even tastier and look fantastic with sweet, long, pointed peppers. The trick here is to make sure all the stock has been absorbed before adding another ladleful – it's definitely worth the wait.

Serves 4-6
Ready in 40 minutes

1 Put the chicken breasts in a saucepan and add half of the lemon juice, then cover with 800ml of cold water. Season, bring to the boil, cover and simmer for 10–15 minutes, until the chicken is thoroughly cooked. Drain, reserving the cooking water to use as stock and slice the chicken breasts.

2 Meanwhile, heat the olive oil in a large saucepan and sauté the garlic and onion, for 2 minutes, until softened. Add the rice and cook, stirring, for 2 minutes, coating the rice completely. Add the peppers, mushrooms and white wine, cooking until the wine evaporates.

3 Add a ladle of the stock made in step 1 and simmer, stirring, until the liquid has been absorbed. Continue the process until all the stock has been added. This will take around 15 minutes. Stir in the cooked chicken, lemon zest and juice, parsley and Parmesan, then season with black pepper. Simmer for 5 minutes, until the chicken is piping hot, then serve, garnished with parsley.

2 skinless chicken breasts
Zest and juice of 1 lemon
2 tbsp olive oil
1 clove of garlic, crushed
1 onion, finely chopped
300g Arborio rice
4 various colour pointed peppers, deseeded and quartered lengthways
200g any mushrooms, sliced
50ml white wine
7g fresh flat leaf parsley, chopped, plus extra to garnish
75g Parmesan, grated
Salt and black pepper

By Liz O'Keefe

Beef stroganoff

This speciality from Eastern Europe just wouldn't be the same without those key peppers. We have used mini sweet peppers in this recipe, for a chunky and flavourful change.

Serves 4
Ready in 35 minute

1 In a large saucepan, heat the oil and fry the sirloin and onions for 2 minutes. Stir in 500ml of water and the mushrooms, cover and stew for 3 minutes, or until soft. Add the peppers and gherkins, and cook, covered, for 3–5 minutes, until softened.

2 In a small bowl, blend the tomato purée with the cream, flour, sweet paprika and 2 tbsp of the sirloin juices from the saucepan, then add the mixture back into the pan. Bring to the boil and simmer for 10–15 minutes, until reduced. Serve with potatoes, rice or bread.

3 tbsp vegetable oil
500g sirloin steak, sliced
3 onions, chopped
500g button mushrooms, whole
500g mini sweet peppers, deseeded and halved lengthways
3 gherkins, drained and chopped
1 tbsp sweet paprika
4 tbsp tomato purée
110ml single cream
3 tbsp plain flour
7g fresh flat leaf parsley, chopped
Salt and black pepper
Boiled potatoes, steamed rice or bread, to serve

By Monika Miecznikowska, Valley Grown Nurseries crop analyst

Red pepper pasta (v)

Making pasta is simple once you know how – and with this recipe, you don't even need a pasta machine. Once you master the recipe, you can make the most of any fresh ingredients by putting together your own creations.

Serves 4
Ready in 30 minutes

1 In a small blender or with a hand-held blender in a small bowl, liquidize the red pepper and garlic with a third of the oil. In a jug, whisk the eggs and red pepper mixture together and then place the flour in a large bowl. Make a well in the middle of the flour by twisting a wooden spoon around and pour the egg mixture into it.

2 Using a fork, whisk the flour into the egg mixture from the outside in, until the mixture comes together, then bring the mixture to a ball with your hands. On a lightly floured surface, knead the pasta dough until firm, smooth and glossy. Re-coat the surface with flour, then divide the dough into eight pieces.

3 Lay out a clean, damp tea towel on another work surface, and rest all but one dough ball on it. Roll the one ball out as far as it will go with a flour-dusted rolling pin, so the pasta is very thin, and then with a sharp knife, slice into strips. Place onto the tea towel and repeat as swiftly as you can with the remaining pasta dough balls.

4 In a large saucepan, cook the pasta in boiling water for 3-5 minutes, drain and refresh. Coat the pasta with the remaining olive oil and lemon zest and juice, olives, capers, basil, Parmesan and nutmeg, and season with salt and crushed pink peppercorns. Divide between four warmed plates and serve immediately.

1 red bell pepper, deseeded and chopped
1 clove of garlic, crushed
3 tbsp extra virgin olive oil
4 eggs
400g plain or '00' flour, sifted
Zest and juice of ½ lemon
100g pitted black olives
1 tsp capers
7g fresh basil, roughly torn
50g Parmesan shavings
½ tsp freshly grated nutmeg
Sea salt and pink peppercorns

By Liz O'Keefe

Lamb sosaties

Give this South African classic a go this spring with the traditional meat of choice, lamb. These kebabs also bring something out of the ordinary to your summer barbecue.

Serves 4
Ready in 25 minutes, plus marinating

1 For the marinade, heat the olive oil in a large saucepan and sauté the onions and garlic for 4 minutes. Mix in the apricot jam, curry powder, cumin, sugar and stock to the saucepan. Bring to the boil and simmer for 5 minutes, until reduced and glossy.

2 Place the crushed bay leaves, lamb and apricots in a large heatproof dish, then pour the marinade over. Cover with tin foil and allow to cool before chilling overnight, or at least 2 hours, turning 3-4 times to continue to coat.

3 Thread the lamb, apricots and peppers onto the skewers, them cook on the grill for 10-15 minutes, turning occasionally. Serve with new potatoes and salad.

3 tbsp olive oil

2 onions, chopped

3 cloves of garlic, crushed

2 tbsp apricot jam

1 tsp cumin

1 tbsp brown sugar

100ml vegetable stock

3 bay leaves, crushed

800g lamb leg steak, cut into cubes

16 dried apricots

4 pointed red peppers, deseeded and sliced into rings

You will also need:

8 wooden skewers, soaked in water for 20 minutes and drained

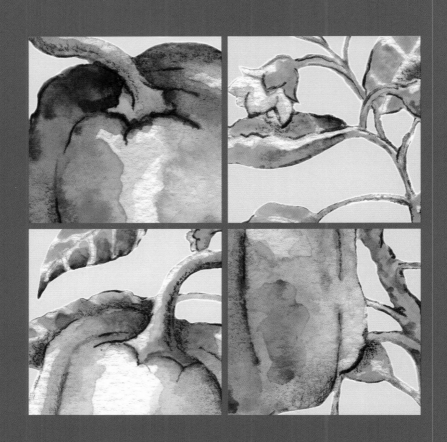

Posh Pepper Recipes

Beef and pepper Wellington

Jazz up an already spectacular dinner party centrepiece with some wilted multi-coloured bell peppers wrapped around the fillet steak. With a little care and time, this really does make the perfect feast.

Serves 8-10
Ready in 1 hour 15 minutes, plus chilling time

1 Preheat the grill, then arrange the pepper quarters on the grill tray, skin up. Coat with a third of the oil and the sugar. Cook until they blister, then squeeze over the lemon and season. Cover and chill for 5 minutes.

2 Preheat the oven to 220C/gas 7 and grease a baking tray. Trim the beef fillet to a more uniform rectangular shape, if necessary, and sit it on a different roasting tray. Brush with 1 tbsp of the remaining olive oil and season with pepper, then roast for 10 minutes for rare, 15 minutes for medium-rare or 20 minutes for medium.

3 Overlap two pieces of cling film over a large chopping board. Lay the pepper slices slightly overlapping, on top, and place the fillet on top of that. Wrap the peppers around the fillet, using the cling film, and chill for 20 minutes.

4 In a frying pan, heat the remaining oil and the butter until bubbling. Add the mushrooms and sauté for 5 minutes, until soft. Stir in the Gorgonzola and thyme, then pour in the sherry. Bring to the boil and then cook for 2 minutes or until the liquid is reduced by half. Blend the mushroom mixture into a rough paste in a food processor or in a bowl with a hand-held blender.

- 6 various colour bell peppers, deseeded and quartered
- 3 tbsp olive oil
- ½ tsp sugar
- Juice of ½ lemon
- 25g butter, plus extra for greasing
- 1kg fillet steak
- 250g mixed wild or chestnut mushrooms, finely chopped
- 50g Gorgonzola, crumbled
- 1 tbsp fresh thyme leaves
- 50ml sherry or white wine
- Plain flour, for dusting
- 450g puff pastry (see *Make puff pastry* opposite to make your own)
- 1 egg yolk, beaten
- Black pepper
- Steamed green beans or spinach, to serve

5 On a clean surface, lightly dusted with flour, roll out a third of the pastry into a rectangle slightly bigger than the fillet and place on the prepared baking tin. Roll the remaining pastry out to double the size, width-wise. Spread the pastry on the tin with a third of the mushroom mixture, leaving about a thumb-width border. Unroll the pepper-covered fillet out of its cling film and onto the mushroom mixture. Spread the remaining mushroom mixture onto the other piece of pastry, leaving a border of around two thumb-widths all the way around, and place, mushroom-side down, on top of the fillet. Press the sides of the pastry down together to seal, using dabs of cold water to fix, then trim the pastry and make a pattern around the edge with the back of a fork. Chill for 10 minutes.

6 Brush with the beaten egg yolk, then bake for 15–20 minutes, until golden, the serve after resting for 5 minutes.

By Liz O'Keefe

Make puff pastry

To make your own puff pastry, sieve 250g plain flour into a large bowl and add a pinch of sea salt. Mix in 250g chilled butter cubes until they are all covered with flour. Pour in enough water to bring the mixture to a dough (adding it a couple of tablespoons at a time). On a surface dusted with flour, roll the pastry out to a rectangle shape then mark it with the rolling pin, into three equal quarters. Fold each side over each other into the middle, then turn the square 90°, so the folds in the pastry face you, and repeat the rolling and folding process four times. Wrap in cling film and chill for 20 minutes.

Sweet potato, roasted pepper and chorizo loaf

TV baker Miranda Gore Browne has shared her unbelievably tasty savoury cake loaf, with roasted red peppers in the mix. As well as being quick and easy to make, this is a versatile recipe that can be served as a starter or with a meal.

Makes 1 loaf
Ready in 50 minutes

1 Preheat the oven to 170C/gas 3 and line a 2lb loaf tin with non-stick baking paper or use a loaf tin liner.

2 Prick the skin of the sweet potatoes with a fork and then put them on a plate in the microwave and cook on high heat for about 10 minutes. Slice in half and use a metal spoon to scrape the flesh out into a bowl. Alternatively, peel, chop and cook the sweet potatoes in boiling water for about 10 minutes until soft and then drain. Mash with a fork in a large bowl.

3 Heat 1 tablespoon of the olive oil in a pan and gently fry the chorizo until crisp. Set aside.

4 Add the eggs and remaining oil to the sweet potato then stir in the dry ingredients. Add the peppers, chorizo and the spicy oil you fried it in to the mixture, reserving about 6 slices to put on top of the loaf at the end. Mix well to combine.

5 Scrape into the prepared tin and top with the reserved chorizo slices and a sprinkling of mixed seeds. Bake in the preheated oven for about 30–35 minutes or until a skewer inserted into the centre comes out clean. Leave to cool in the tin, then serve.

Ingredients

- 300g sweet potato
- 80ml olive oil (or use the oil from the peppers)
- 150g chorizo, finely sliced
- 2 large eggs
- 150g self-raising flour (or 100g self-raising flour and 50g wholemeal plain flour)
- 1 tsp bicarbonate of soda
- ½ tsp salt
- 2 tsp paprika
- 100g roasted bell peppers in oil, drained and chopped (see page 24 for roasting instructions)
- Handful of mixed seeds, for sprinkling

Tip

This is delicious eaten warm with soup or strong cheese and chutney. You can also make a great vegetarian version by simply leaving out the chorizo.

Recipe taken from
Bake Me a Cake as Fast as You Can
by Miranda Gore Browne (Ebury Press)

Mini pepper and vegetable tempura with sweet chilli sauce

A Japanese dish, tempura basically means coating something in a light, fluffy batter and you can pretty much tempura any vegetable – with mini sweet peppers being the best! Serve with our quick chilli jam or simply soy sauce, as a dinner party starter or party food.

Serves 4-6
Ready in 30 minutes

1 To make the batter, whisk the flours, baking powder, paprika, water, salt and coriander together, until the mixture is combined and smooth. Chill for 10 minutes.

2 Meanwhile, to make the chilli jam, place the chilli and its seeds, sugar, vinegar and lemon juice in a saucepan and bring to the boil. Keep on a rolling boil for 5 minutes, or until thick. Pour into a serving bowl.

3 Dry the peppers, courgettes, broccoli and sweet potato with kitchen towel and dust with flour in a large bowl (or a couple of large bowls) so the vegetables are completely covered.

4 Meanwhile, heat enough oil in a wok to cover the vegetables. When the oil is sizzling (you can test by dropping a little bit of the batter into the oil and if it sizzles, the oil is ready), dip batches of the vegetables in the batter before immediately adding them to the oil. Cook for 1-2 minutes, turn, and cook for a further 1-2 minutes or until the batter is lightly browned. Drain on kitchen paper to remove any excess oil and keep warm. Serve immediately with the chilli jam or soy sauce.

400g plain flour, sifted, plus extra for dusting

100g cornflour

2 tbsp baking powder

1 tbsp paprika

200ml sparkling water

Pinch of sea salt

4g fresh coriander, very finely chopped

4 red chillies, chopped

4 tbsp sugar

120ml white wine vinegar

Juice of 1 lemon

500g mini sweet peppers

2 red pointed peppers, deseeded and halved lengthways

2 courgettes, roughly cut into sticks

1 broccoli head, separated into large florets

1 sweet potato, peeled and roughly cut into sticks

Sunflower oil, to shallow fry

Tip

 Fry the same vegetable in each batch to ensure even cooking.

By Liz O'Keefe

Moroccan mutton and pepper tagine

Peppers are essential in Moroccan cuisine and add to that rich depth of flavours the African country is known for. We have made the most of lesser-used mutton for this slow-cooking dish that is well worth the wait.

Serves 4
Ready in 2 hours

1 Preheat the oven to 160C/gas 3. Combine the flour, turmeric, paprika and cayenne pepper in a mixing bowl and coat the mutton in it.

2 In a tagine, if using, or a large saucepan, heat the oil and sauté the onions and garlic for 5–8 minutes, until very soft. Remove any excess flour from the mutton and add it into the frying pan, browning on all sides, then stir in the peppers, tomato purée and ginger. Cook for a further 2 minutes, then add the tomatoes, dried apricots and almonds.

3 Transfer to a casserole dish if not using a tagine and season with salt and pepper and add the saffron. Cover with boiling water and stir well, then place in the oven for 1 hour 30 minutes. Check and stir after 1 hour, adding a little water if the sauce is too dry. Serve with couscous and yogurt.

2 tbsp plain flour

3 tsp turmeric

3 tsp paprika

1 tsp cayenne pepper

600g mutton, diced

4 tbsp olive oil

2 onions, chopped

2 cloves of garlic, sliced

2 green bell peppers and 2 red pointed peppers, deseeded and sliced lengthways

2 tbsp tomato purée

1cm piece fresh root ginger, grated

4 tomatoes, blanched, deseeded and chopped (see page 38 for blanching tips)

100g dried apricots

3 tbsp flaked almonds, plus extra to garnish

Pinch of saffron

Salt and white pepper

Couscous and yogurt, to serve

Seafood and peppers in black bean sauce

Wow guests by making this classic Chinese combination from scratch. And, once you've made this – you can have a go at making the Brazilian black bean soup on page 54 with the leftover black beans.

Serves 4
Ready in 25 minutes

1 To make the black bean sauce: In a saucepan, heat half the oil and fry the black beans for 3 minutes until warmed through completely.

2 In a separate bowl, mix the cornflour with 1 tbsp cold water to make a paste. Mix in the soy sauce, sherry and honey, then add to the black beans. Stir 150ml boiling water in gradually and bring to the boil, stirring constantly. Simmer for 5–10 minutes until thick and set aside until needed.

3 Heat a wok or large saucepan until hot, and then add the remaining oil. Stir in the garlic, peppers and spring onions and fry for 2 minutes. Add the seafood and black bean sauce, and cook for 3-4 minutes until the seafood is piping hot. Season with pepper and serve.

Tip

Bulk make the black bean sauce by increasing by four all the ingredients in steps 1 and 2, then freeze in portions for another day.

4 tsp vegetable oil

100g tin black beans, rinsed and drained

1 tbsp cornflour

1 tbsp dark soy sauce

75ml sherry or dry white wine

1 tbsp honey

1 clove of garlic, sliced

3 red and/or orange bell peppers, deseeded and diced

6 spring onions, trimmed and chopped

500g cooked mixed seafood

Black pepper

Steamed rice or egg noodles, to serve

By Liz O'Keefe

Scottish pepper, potato and black pudding breakfast stack

How do you like your eggs in the morning? Food writer Gregor McMaster likes his with peppers and soon so will you, with this hearty breakfast stack.

Serves 4
Ready in 35 minutes

1 Preheat the oven to 180C/gas 4. In a bowl, toss together the potatoes, oil and Parmesan. Line a baking sheet with baking paper and arrange the potato slices in a single layer. Bake for 20–25 minutes until crisp. Keep warm in the turned-off oven (with the door slightly open).

2 Heat the butter in a large frying pan and cook the black pudding for 3 minutes, turn over and add the peppers. Cook for 3 minutes, turning once, until the peppers are softened. On four serving plates, loosely layer the cooked potatoes, black pudding and peppers to create a tower.

3 To poach the eggs, bring a large pan of water to the boil and break each egg into it, moving each over slightly, helping it form. Bring to the boil and then simmer immediately. Cook to your liking before removing with a slotted spoon and topping each stack with one. Season with pepper and serve immediately.

2 large maris piper potatoes, sliced

2 tsp olive oil

2 tbsp Parmesan, finely grated

15g butter

8 thin slices of black pudding

1 yellow, 1 red and 1 green bell pepper, roasted, peeled and quartered

4 eggs, at room temperature

Black pepper

By Gregor McMaster

Stuffed padron peppers (Bharela Marcha) (V)

Food writer 'the Botanical Baker', Urvashi Roe has shared an adaptation of her mother's traditional Gujarati recipe, Bharela Marcha. The recipe traditionally uses bullet chillies, which have been replaced with padron peppers, and a garnish of coconut and coriander has been added.

Serves 2
Ready in 30 minutes

1 To prepare the peppers, trim the stalks and slit each one lengthways, taking care not to cut in half, and scoop out all the seeds. Pop them into a bowl and cover with cold water for 10 minutes.

2 Meanwhile, toast the cumin and coriander seeds in a frying pan until they start to turn slightly brown. Toss them into a pestle and mortar and grind them down to a powder. Add the chickpea flour to the frying pan and lightly toast for 3 minutes until it gives off a nutty aroma and starts to turn darker. Add the toasted flour to the ground toasted seeds, add in the sugar and salt, and then mix until well combined. Stir in the lemon juice and half the oil. Divide the mixture between each pepper cavity.

3 Heat the remaining oil in a saucepan and test if it ready to use by adding a mustard seed. If the seed fizzles and pops then it's good to go. Add the mustard seeds, let them fizzle and pop for 30 seconds to release their flavour and then immediately turn the heat to low. Add each stuffed pepper one by one into the oil and then stir gently to coat each one evenly in the oil. Add 2 tbsp of cold water, cover and leave to cook for 10-15 minutes, until cooked through.

4 In the meantime, prepare the coconut garnish by putting the desiccated coconut into a bowl. Pour over some hot water and leave for 5 minutes, then drain and squeeze out any excess water. Add the tomatoes and chopped coriander and mix together. Serve with the peppers.

12 padron, jalapeno or mini sweet peppers
2 tbsp cumin seeds
2 tbsp coriander seeds
3 tbsp chickpea flour (gram flour)
3 tbsp soft brown sugar
1 tsp salt
Juice of 1 lemon
4 tbsp vegetable oil
1 tsp small black mustard seeds
2 tbsp desiccated coconut
2 medium-sized tomatoes, cubed
40g fresh coriander, chopped

By Urvashi Roe

Red pepper damper bread

Traditionally baked in the ashes of a campfire and eaten with golden syrup, damper bread is a classic Australian soda bread that has transformed into many different variations since its origins in the outback. We have mixed some red peppers and pink peppercorns into the dough – this tastes great with a dollop of mascarpone.

Serves 4
Ready in 55 minutes

1 Preheat the oven to 200C/gas 6 and grease a flat baking tray. Combine the flour, salt and sugar in a large mixing bowl. Using your hands, rub in the butter until the mixture has the consistency of fine breadcrumbs. Add the chopped red peppers and pink peppercorns.

2 Mix in the milk slowly to make a soft dough. Lightly knead the dough on a surface lightly dusted with flour for 2–3 minutes. Shape the dough into a round loaf and transfer it to the baking tray. Brush with the extra milk and score a cross into the top with a sharp knife.

3 Bake for 30 minutes or until it sounds hollow when you gently tap it on the top with the back of a spoon. Cool on a wire rack and then serve with butter or mascarpone.

80g butter, plus extra for greasing
450g self-raising flour, sifted
1 tsp salt
1 tsp caster sugar
2 red bell peppers, deseeded and chopped
1 tbsp ground pink peppercorns
180ml milk, plus extra for brushing

Seared lamb, lentil and roasted red pepper salad with salsa verde

Here, food writer Lucy Blackwell shares her filling warm pepper salad recipe and shows us how to serve the perfect lamb steak.

Serves 2
Ready in 40 minutes, plus resting time

1 Preheat the grill. Arrange the pepper quarters, skin up, on a baking tray. Grill until the skins blister, then transfer to a bowl, cover with cling film and set aside.

2 Combine the red onion, caster sugar and 1 tbsp of the red wine vinegar in a bowl. Season with salt and set aside. Place the lentils in a saucepan and cover with cold water. Bring to the boil, add the bouillon powder and simmer for 15-20 minutes, until tender and drain. Take the lamb out of the fridge now, so it can come up to room temperature for around 20 minutes. This will ensure it doesn't tense up in the hot pan and cooks evenly.

3 Meanwhile, to make the salsa verde dressing, blend the flat-leaf parsley, basil, anchovy fillets, capers, garlic, extra virgin olive oil, lemon zest and juice, and the remaining red wine vinegar in a food processor until almost smooth, then season with salt and pepper.

4 Peel and slice the peppers, then heat the olive oil in a large frying pan over a high heat until very hot. Season the lamb with pepper and fry for 2½ minutes on each side or until cooked to your liking. Transfer to a board, season with salt and cover loosely with foil. Leave to rest for 3 minutes.

5 Divide the drained lentils between two serving plates. Top with the pepper slices, red onion and salad leaves. Thinly slice the lamb and add to the plates. Drizzle over the salsa verde dressing and serve.

Tip

The recipe makes more dressing than is needed, but leftovers will keep in a screw-top jar in the fridge for up to 3 days. Drizzle over griddled chicken and steamed fish, or use to dress boiled potatoes or vegetables just before serving.

1 red bell pepper, deseeded and quartered
¼ red onion, thinly sliced
¼ tsp caster sugar
2 tbsp red wine vinegar
80g green lentils, rinsed
½ tsp vegetable bouillon
2 lamb leg steaks
15g each fresh flat-leaf parsley and basil, chopped
2 anchovy fillets in oil, drained
1 tbsp capers, rinsed and drained
1 garlic clove, peeled
6 tbsp extra virgin olive oil
Zest and juice of 1 lemon
1 tbsp olive oil
50g mixed salad leaves
Salt and black pepper

By Lucy Blackwell

Squash and pepper stacks

Here the Vegetarian Society does what it does best and proves that, with a little help from the pepper, that veggie can be posh.

Serves 4
Ready in 30 minutes

1 Place the rice in a saucepan and cover with cold water. Bring the rice to the boil, then simmer for 20-25 minutes, until al dente.

2 In a large saucepan, heat half of the olive oil and sauté the onion for 4-5 minutes, until soft and starting to caramelize. Add the cardamom seeds, allspice and raisins, and cook for 2 minutes. Mix in the cooked rice, feta and parsley.

3 Preheat the oven to 140C/gas 1. In a separate saucepan, parboil the butternut squash circles in boiling water for 2-3 minutes, or until slightly softened. In a small bowl, mix the remaining 1 tbsp oil with the vinegar, then coat the squash and peppers with it. Heat a griddle pan and chargrill the squash and peppers for 2-3 minutes on each side. Place the squash and peppers on a baking tray and keep warm in the oven. In a small saucepan, melt the cranberry sauce with 1 tbsp water.

4 To assemble the stacks, place one squash circle in the centre of a dinner plate. Place an 8.5cm ring over/on top of it and press in a quarter of the rice mixture. On top of this place a second circle and decoratively pile a quarter of the grilled peppers. To finish, drizzle over the cranberry sauce.

175g Camargue red rice

2 tbsp light olive oil

150g red onion, finely chopped

½ tsp cardamom seeds

½ tsp allspice

1½ tbsp raisins

100g vegetarian feta cheese, diced

7g fresh flat leaf parsley, finely chopped

½ butternut squash (the top end), peeled and cut into 8 circles

1 tbsp balsamic vinegar

2 red bell peppers, cut into 8 thick slices

100g cranberry sauce

By The Vegetarian Society

Fried squid with romesco sauce and pepper croutons

Treat yourself with supper club pop-up creator, Rosie Llewellyn's version of the classic Catalonian romesco sauce with delicately fried squid and red pepper croutons.

Serves 2
Ready in 1 hour 20 minutes

1 Preheat the oven to 200C/gas 6. Lay the flaked almonds on a dry roasting tin and roast for 5 minutes. Transfer to a plate and set aside, keeping the oven on. Put the pepper, tomatoes and garlic into the roasting tray, sprinkle over the cayenne pepper and half the paprika, then drizzle with one third of the olive oil. Roast for 25 minutes, then add half of the bread and roast for 5 minutes. Leave the oven on.

2 Squeeze the roast garlic out of its skins into a food processor and add the roasted bread, pepper and tomatoes, roasted almonds and three-quarters of the vinegar and blitz until nearly smooth. Transfer 1 tbsp to a bowl, then add the remaining bread and bake on a tray for 20 minutes, turning half way through, to make the croutons.

3 Meanwhile, to make the dressing, place the black olives, 1 tbsp of the olive oil and the remaining red wine vinegar in a food processor and blitz until smooth.

4 Combine the remaining paprika, the flour and ground almonds on a plate and season. Add the squid, coating well. Heat the remaining oil in a pan over a medium–high heat and add the squid. Cook for 2 minutes, or until the tentacles start to curl. Divide the sauce and squid between two plates. Add rocket leaves and a few croutons, then drizzle each with the dressing. Serve.

Tip

To prepare the squid, remove the long plastic-looking spine by pinching it out and remove the guts by reaching inside and feeling for anything that's not the outer flesh. Wash the squid, then chop into 2cm rings, leaving the tentacles whole. You can ask your fishmonger to do it for you, or buy fresh raw squid rings.

2 tbsp flaked almonds

1 red bell pepper, deseeded and quartered

6 cherry tomatoes, halved

6 large cloves of garlic

3 tbsp olive oil

Pinch of cayenne pepper

2 tsp paprika

2 stale slices of white bread, cut into cubes

4 tsp red wine vinegar

2 tbsp black olives

1 tbsp plain flour

2 tsp ground almonds

3 whole squid, cleaned, gutted and sliced into rings and tentacle pieces (see tip)

100g rocket leaves

Salt and black pepper

By Rosie Llewellyn

Tofu and spinach stuffed pepper curry (v)

Food writer Deena Kakaya loves mini sweet peppers and has teamed them up with some bold, spicy flavours and a homemade cashew cream in this sweet curry.

Serves 2-4
Ready in 1 hour

1 Slit the peppers lengthways and remove the seeds. Set aside. Wrap the tofu block up in kitchen paper to remove any excess moisture and also set aside. In a small bowl, cover the cashew nuts with milk and leave to soak for 20 minutes.

2 Preheat the oven to at 190C/gas 5. Heat two-thirds of the oil in a saucepan and add half of the cumin seeds. Once the seeds sizzle, add the onion, a pinch of salt and turmeric, and sauté until soften. Scramble the tofu by crushing it in your hands and adding it to the pan. Stir in the paprika, ground coriander and chilli powder, before adding the spinach. Cook on low for 5 minutes, then cool to room temperature. Stuff the peppers evenly with the cooled mixture and place in a roasting tin. Roast for 35-40 minutes, covering with tin foil halfway through.

3 In the meantime, make the curry base by blitzing the cashew nuts, reserving the milk, to a smooth paste in a food processor or with a hand held blender in a bowl. When a paste, blend in the reserved milk.

4 Heat the remaining oil in a wok or large saucepan, then add the remaining cumin seeds, cardamom pods, cloves, cinnamon, chillies and curry leaves. Allow the seeds to sizzle before turning the heat down and stirring in the garlic. Sauté the garlic for 30 seconds, before adding the cashew nut cream and 300ml of cold water. Simmer for 5-8 minutes, until thickened. Pour the sauce into a shallow dish and top with the roast peppers. Serve with rice or breads.

10 mini sweet peppers
150g firm tofu, drained
3 tbsp cashew nuts
3 tbsp milk
3 tbsp vegetable oil
2 tsp cumin seeds
1 red onion, finely chopped
½ tsp turmeric
½ tsp paprika
1 tsp ground coriander
Pinch of chilli powder
150g spinach, very finely chopped
2-3 cardamom pods
2-3 cloves
1 stick of cinnamon
3 green chillies
6 curry leaves
2 cloves of garlic, minced or very finely chopped
Salt
Rice or breads, to serve

By Deena Kakaya

Beef and pepper bunny chow

A popular street food in South Africa, bunny chow is a tasty snack in a bread bun. Food writer Gregor McMaster shares his dinner-sized version, which includes an array of multi-coloured bell peppers.

Serves 4
Ready in 2 hours 15 minutes

1 In a large pan, heat 2 tbsp of the oil and add the beef, frying until browned. You may need to do this in batches. Remove with a slotted spoon and set aside.

2 Sauté the shallots in the same pan for 2–3 minutes, or until soft. Add garlic and cook for 2 minutes, then stir in the curry paste, crushed chillies, cinnamon and star anise and cook for 2 minutes. Return the beef to the pan, stir to coat and pour over the beef stock and wine. Gently simmer covered for 1 hour 20 minutes.

3 Heat the remaining tbsp of oil in a frying pan and fry one of the red peppers and the green pepper and the sweet potato for 5 minutes. Stir into the meat and cook for a further 30 minutes. Meanwhile, dry fry the chorizo in the frying pan and set aside.

4 Serve the curry in the remaining red pepper bread rolls topped with the chorizo, cherry tomatoes, sour cream and coriander.

3 tbsp vegetable oil
500g stewing beef, chopped
2 shallots, diced
2 cloves of garlic, crushed
2 tbsp red curry paste
½ tbsp crushed chillies
½ tsp cinnamon
1 star anise
250ml beef stock
100ml Pinotage or another red wine
2 red and 1 yellow bell pepper, deseeded and sliced
1 sweet potato, peeled and cubed
50g chorizo, chopped
4 small bread rolls, hollowed out
100g cherry tomatoes, quartered
50ml sour cream
4g fresh coriander, chopped

By Gregor McMaster

Fillet steak with pepper cream sauce

Learn how to cook one of the more tender steaks around and enjoy it with a creamy pepper sauce that will have you making more and more.

Serves 2
Ready in 30 minutes

1 Remove the steaks from the fridge to come up to room temperature. This is especially important if you are cooking them rare as the uncooked meat in the middle needs to be warm, not cold.

2 Meanwhile, heat the butter until sizzling and then mix in the oil and then sauté the garlic and shallot for 2-3 minutes, until softened. Add the peppers and sauté for 2 minutes. Mix in the honey and season with salt and pepper. Stir in the white wine and bring to the boil. Simmer for 5 minutes, or until reduced by half. Transfer to a food processor and blend into a fine paste, or purée in a bowl with a hand-held blender. Return to the pan and set aside.

3 Heat a griddle pan on a high heat or heat a little oil in a frying pan. Add the fillet steaks, flat-side down, and turn over after 1 minute (or until little finger's width colours from the heat) for rare, 1½ minutes (one and a half little finger's width) for medium and 2 minutes or coloured just about one third of the way up for well done. Repeat the cooking times for the other side then, pick each up with tongs, sealing the fillets all the way round by pushing it up against the griddle/pan. Place on a plate and cover with tin foil to rest for 5 minutes.

4 In the meantime, return the pepper sauce to the heat and warm through. Stir in the lemon juice and zest, and simmer for 30 seconds. Off the heat, stir through the tarragon and crème fraiche. Serve with the fillet steaks, along with seasonal vegetables and chips.

2 x 150g fillet steaks
50g butter
1 tsp olive oil
1 clove of garlic, finely chopped
1 shallot, finely chopped
4 red bell peppers, deseeded and chopped
1 tsp honey
125ml white wine
Zest and juice of ½ lemon
4g fresh tarragon, chopped
40ml crème fraiche
Sea salt and black pepper
Seasonal vegetables and chips, to serve

By Liz O'Keefe

Red pepper, lemon and coriander focaccia

An Italian favourite, focaccia is the best way to show off your bread-making skills. Delicate and fragrant, this red pepper, lemon and coriander combination is a fresh and zingy accompaniment to an alfresco meal, or good party food with extra oil and vinegars to dip in.

Makes 1 loaf
Ready in 1 hour, plus resting

1 In a large bowl, combine the flour and a pinch of salt. Make a well in the middle of the flour and sprinkle the yeast into it. In a small jug, combine 300ml warm water and two-thirds of the oil, then pour into the well in the flour. Stir the flour into the liquid in a circle of eight motion, until a dough forms.

2 Dust your hands with flour then knead the dough for 5 minutes, with in the bowl, adding further flour if needed. Knead in the peppers, coriander and the zest of the lemon, as well as half the pink peppercorns and fennel seeds. Cover with a clean tea towel and place in a warm place to prove for 30 minutes.

3 Meanwhile, grease a rectangular flat baking tray and peel and slice half the lemon, and then quarter the slices, and then halve those quarters so you have small triangles.

4 Preheat the oven to 220C/gas 7. Knock back the dough, by pushing the air out of it with your fist. On a surface lightly dusted with flour, knead for 5 minutes, then knead in all but six of the lemon triangles. Stretch the dough out to fit the prepared tray, then push about six spaced-out dents into the bread with your thumb. Sprinkle with the remaining pink peppercorns and fennel seeds, and sea salt, then place a lemon triangle in each dent. Drizzle with the remaining oil, cover with the tea towel and leave to prove for 15 minutes.

5 Bake for 20–25 minutes, until risen and golden. Garnish with the reserved coriander and extra oil and cut into squares. Serve.

500g strong white flour, plus extra for dusting

7g fast-action yeast

3 tbsp extra virgin olive oil, plus extra for greasing and drizzling

2 red bell peppers, deseeded and finely chopped

7g fresh coriander, chopped, reserving some for garnish

1 lemon

2 tsp pink peppercorns, crushed

2 tsp fennel seeds, crushed

Sea salt

By Liz O'Keefe

Roasted lamuyo pepper with chorizo and garlic toast tapas

This tasty treat from supermarket Tesco makes the most of its line of Finest Lamuyo peppers, which are not as sweet or large as the more common bell pepper. It's the perfect accompaniment for the strong-tasting chorizo and anchovies.

Serves 6
Ready in 50 minutes

1 Heat the oven to 200C/gas 6. Put the peppers and garlic in a roasting dish and coat with the olive oil. Roast for 15–20 minutes until the peppers are darkened on the outside. Transfer the peppers and garlic to a large bowl and reserve the juices in a small bowl.

2 Cover the peppers and garlic with cling film and stand for 15 minutes. Squeeze the garlic out of its skin and into a small bowl. Mash with some black pepper to make a paste and mix in the butter. Set aside. Remove the tops, skin and seeds from the peppers, and tear each into strips. Mix the strips into the reserved juices.

3 Dry-fry the chorizo in a non-stick pan until crisp, then add the pepper mixture, chorizo and chopped parsley, and mix well. Chargrill or grill the bread on both sides, then butter with the garlic butter and top with the peppers. Add a couple of anchovies to each piece of toast then serve.

Tip

Fancy creating a tapas meal? Serve this with the Rare tuna 'au poivre' and piperade tapas (page 100), the Goat's cheese, walnut and chicory salad with yellow pepper dressing (page 46) and the Stuffed padron peppers (page 89).

2 Finest Lamuyo Peppers
1 garlic bulb, halved lengthways
2 tbsp olive oil
60g butter, softened
150g chorizo, sliced
6 slices white crusty bread or sourdough
7g fresh flat-leaf parsley, chopped
12 large white marinated anchovies
Black pepper

By Tesco

Rare tuna 'au poivre' and piperade tapas

This piperade-based tapas from London-based chef Tam Storrar celebrates the sweetness chargrilled peppers bring to a dish, whilst the peppery rare tuna adds both heat and texture.

Serves 4
Ready in 25 minutes

1 Preheat a griddle pan and blister the skins of the peppers, then place in a bowl and cover with cling film. Stand for 5 minutes, then deseed, remove the skins and slice very thinly.

2 To make the piperade, sweat the garlic and shallots in the olive oil in a saucepan, until very soft, then add the piment d'espillete or paprika. Add the sugar, vinegar and passata and reduce until fairly dry and concentrated. This will take around 5-10 minutes. Add the sliced peppers from step 1 and season.

3 Meanwhile, in a sieve, shake all the dust from the cracked pepper, then push the cracked pepper against one side of tuna and season with salt. Always use the salt after the pepper, otherwise the salt draws the moisture out of the pepper and all the pepper falls off during cooking. Heat a heavy-bottomed frying pan until quite hot, then add the groundnut oil. Place the tuna in pan, pepper side down, and fry for 1 minute, then briefly seal the other sides for no more than 10 seconds each side.

4 Rest the tuna for 2 minutes, keeping the pan on the heat, but turning it to low. Flambé with the brandy or cognac and add the chicken stock, reducing for 2 minutes. Season with salt and stir in the lemon juice and butter. Slice the tuna, then divide the broccoli, piperade and the sliced tuna between the four plates and dress with the brandy sauce. Serve with bread and goat's cheese and chicory salad (page 46).

2 red bell peppers and 1 green

2 cloves of garlic, finely sliced

2 banana shallots, finely sliced lengthways

1 tbsp extra virgin olive oil

Pinch of piment d'espelette or paprika

Pinch of sugar

10ml white wine vinegar (see tips)

300ml passata

2 tbsp black and white peppercorns, roughly cracked

500g tuna steak (see tips)

2 tsp groundnut oil

2 tbsp brandy or cognac

60ml chicken stock

1 tsp lemon juice

1 tsp butter

Sea salt and black pepper

Steamed and then griddled tenderstem or purple spouting broccoli and bread, to serve

Tips Pick a piece of firm, bright tuna, making sure it isn't grey or brown. If possible, ask for sashimi grade, as it will basically be eaten raw.

Adding sugar and vinegar is called a gastric and is used to bring out the sweetness of tomato and pepper-based sauces and soups. If a sauce is lacking in punch, a reduction of vinegar and sugar can often put it right, but just be careful not to make your dish into a sweet and sour.

About the Pepper Technology Group

The Pepper Technology Group (PTG) is an association of pepper growers supplying high-quality produce to all of the major UK supermarkets. There are eighteen grower members, thirteen sponsors and three HDC representatives. Each year member numbers increase and by 2015 we hope to represent every sweet pepper grower in the UK.

The association aims to:

Ensure customer satisfaction by supplying consistently high-quality product

Promote sustainable and effective methods of crop protection

Develop efficient alternative sources of energy and water

Provide consumers with information on peppers

Engage with consumers through the website, printed literature and at various food shows, both locally and nationally

The PTG was initially set up in February 2003 and became official in 2007 with the first meeting taking place on 19 July, 2007. Members of the PTG have more than 100 hectares of sweet peppers and chillies collectively across the UK, which amounts to about 153 million peppers a year.

For more information or to contact the PTG go to:
peppertechnologygroup.co.uk
facebook.com/pepper.technology.group
twitter.com/BritishPeppers

Contributors

The Great British Pepper Cookbook has been made possible through the hard work of many different organisations and individuals. The Pepper Technology Group would like to thank the following contributors:

DR NEAL WARD

After working in several different industries, including computer programming and training as a chef, Neal went back to education and gained a PhD in plant physiology at the University of Reading. He is the technical and systems manager at one of the UK's largest organic pepper growers, Cantelo Nurseries in Somerset. Try out his recipe, Chorizo, yellow pepper and basil penne, on page 43.

JON ASHFORD

Photographer and art director, Jon shot the photoshoot for the 10 main recipe images in *The Great British Pepper Cookbook* (pages 29, 50, 53, 56, 63, 67, 78, 81, 87 and 101). Jon has worked for many high-profile glossy magazines over the last 15 years, including *BBC Good Food*, *Elle Decoration* and *Red*. The recipes were food styled by the wonderfully artistic Maud Eden, with Liz O'Keefe as home economist.

LUCY BLACKWELL

Cookery editor on national women's weekly magazines, *Bella, that's life!*, *Take a Break* and *Take a Break Specials*, Lucy is a food styling assistant, food writer and recipe developer and tester, who previously worked on former Surrey foodie mag *Grub*, as well as national magazines, *Woman & Home*, *Heat* and *Closer*. A graduate of Gloucestershire-based The Gables School of Cookery, Lucy specialises in high-end accessible and achievable cookery and has contributed the recipe Seared lamb, lentil and roasted red pepper salad with salsa verde on page 91.

MIRANDA GORE BROWNE

Based in West Sussex, Miranda shot to fame as a finalist on BBC's *The Great British Bake Off*, and is described by baking guru Mary Berry as 'the iced biscuit queen'. She now has two baking books under her (apron) belt: Biscuit and Bake Me As Fast As You Can. Miranda has contributed a recipe from the latter cookbook to *The Great British Pepper Cookbook* – her Sweet potato, pepper and chorizo loaf, which is on page 82.

JASON FREEDMAN

Pepper grower, Thanet Earth's resident chef, Jason is head chef and owner at Canterbury's The Minnis Restaurant and Bar. He has contributed the Virgin pepper Mary on behalf of Thanet Earth, on page 44.

DEENA KAKAYA

Food writer and cookery class instructor, Deena specialises in vegetarian food with an Indian influence and has written for magazines *BBC Good Food*, *delicious*, *Fork* and *Cook Vegetarian*. Find her recipe for Tofu and spinach stuffed pepper curry on page 94.

ROSIE LLEWELLYN

London-based supper club cook and creator and writer of blog www.alittlelusciousness
.com, Rosie has been writing about her recipes, the restaurants she visits and general
foodie experiences for the last three years and her supper clubs are gaining quite a
reputation. She contributed her Fried squid with romesco sauce and pepper croutons
recipe (page 93) to *The Great British Pepper Cookbook*.

GREGOR MCMASTER

Deputy food editor on foodie monthly supermarket magazine ASDA magazine, Gregor
is a recipe developer and food stylist. He has contributed two recipes to *The Great
British Pepper Cookbook* – Breakfast pepper stack and Beef and pepper bunny chow on
pages 88 and 96.

URVASHI ROE

Known as the Botanical Baker, Urvashi's background is as a florist and whilst falling in
love with flowers and plants, she also became obsessive about their nutritional values and
started her blog thebotanicalbaker.wordpress.com. A food writer and recipe developer,
Urvashi was been a contestant on BBC's *The Great British Bake Off* and contributed her
Stuffed padron peppers recipe on page 89.

TAM STORRAR

Tam Storrar is head chef at Soho Parisian bistro, Blanchette, a project set up by brothers,
Maxime, Yannis and Malik Alary, with the backing of Simon Mullins and Ben Tish of
the Salt Yard Group. Tam has been both Senior Chef de Partie and then Senior Sous
Chef at London restaurant Bibendum and contributed Blanchette's Rare tuna 'au
poivre' and piperade tapas recipe on page 100.

GUUS VREDENBURG

Chef Guus runs the Vredenburg Creatief Culinair (VCC), a culinary consultancy agency
for the food industry, the food and catering industry and related businesses. He has
undertaken recipe design work for the EU Colourful Taste campaign, which aims to
increase pepper consumption, and has contributed the Gazpacho recipe on page 47.

Special thanks to: Charlie Street and James Thompson (Media Street Ltd), John Sivak,
Celia Cozens and Patricia Graham (Libri Publishing), Mike Tapp (recipetips.com), The
Lea Valley Growers' Association, Gerard Vaunk and Zoe Smith (Tangmere Airfield
Nurseries), Gill Wardell, Luke Hibberd and Brian Hibberd (Abbey View Produce Ltd),
Judy Whittaker and Steve Hatt (Thanet Earth), Jeremy Green (Facing Heaven Chilli
Company), Su Taylor (Vegetarian Society), Rosemary Street, Josh Murphy and Random
House.

A big thank you to our sponsors: Tony Girard (koppert), Nick Field (Priva Uk), Tim
Pratt (FEC Services), Jill koojiman (Enza Zaden Seeds), Hugh Lisher (De-Ruiter Seeds),
Stuart Lambert (RijR Zwaan Seeds), James Hatherill (Tozer Seeds), Roger Beard
(Agrovista), Jos Boeters (Hollandplant), Dave Wilson (Plant Raisers), Andrew Lee
(Grodan) and Kim Harding (Cultilene).

Meet the growers

ABBEY VIEW PRODUCE

'The best thing about growing peppers is seeing how they brighten up supermarket displays'

Meet... Brian Hibberd, managing director of Abbey View Produce
Located... Waltham Abbey, Essex
Growing area... 10 acres
Amount grown... 5.2 million bell peppers
Pepper experience... 15 years
Favourite pepper recipe... Pepper crudités with dip

Why grow peppers in the Lea Valley?

The Lea Valley is a great British traditional growing region with established glasshouse area and fantastic transport links into London and around the country.

What's your best pepper growing tip?

For home gardeners, make sure the plant is receiving plenty of light and is kept well watered. Picking a variety with smaller fruit sizes, like a mini sweet, allows quicker ripening and therefore you'll have a bigger and more impressive crop!

What's the best thing about growing peppers?

The best thing about growing peppers is seeing how they brighten up supermarket displays and how consumers enjoy eating them.

How has pepper growing changed over the years?

The main change has been to the recommended height of commercial greenhouses and modernization of growing technics that accompanies this.

If you were to recommend a pepper to cook with, which one would it be?

The pointed Ramiro type is great – grilled, fried or roasted!

Which pepper plant is the best to grow?

Red and yellow pepper plants look amazing mid-summer, with a full fruit load.

What's the best thing that's happened to the British pepper growing industry in the last 10 years?

The development of speciality varieties, such as mini sweet and pointed, along with the public's recognition of the versatility of peppers to add flavour and colour to many dishes, have been the best things to happen.

What's next for pepper growing?

The biggest change for commercial growers will be individual solutions to the growing energy costs via development of green energies, such as anaerobic digestion, heat exchange technologies and renewable fuel sources, like woodchip and straw.

THANET EARTH

'Getting the yields right and dealing with a living crop makes pepper growing the best job in the world'

Meet... Pleun van Malkenhorst, managing director of Rainbow UK Ltd (Thanet Earth)
Located... Isle of Thanet, Kent
Growing area... 22 acres
Amount grown... 16 million bell, pointed and mini sweet peppers
Favourite pepper recipe... Roasted garlic and sweet pepper pasta bake

What's the best thing about growing peppers?

Getting the yields right and dealing with a living crop makes pepper growing the best job in the world. There's a real skill and science behind growing peppers. Whilst the quality of the crop has to be great, getting the plants to be as productive as possible is really important.

Why grow peppers in Thanet?

We're right on the coast, on a peninsula setting and this gives us a superb amount of natural light and outside humidity to help the plants perform as well as possible. The amount of fruit and the speed of ripening is directly related to light levels. We grow 12% of all the peppers grown in the UK.

How do you eat your peppers?

I tend to eat whole bell peppers like apples, and I often roast the sweet pointed peppers as an accompaniment to pretty much any meal. A well-made pepper sauce is superb too, and it's easy to make a large batch and freeze it.

Which is your favourite pepper to grow?

Every pepper variety has its own character and requires a different approach at different times of the year. If I had to pick a personal favourite, it would be the orange bell pepper. It's always such a strong plant with lots of personality!

How did you first get into growing peppers?

I have been growing peppers at Thanet Earth since 2010. Before that I studied Agricultural Business Studies. My roots are in the Westland area of Holland where greenhouse production is a major industry. I grew up working in and around greenhouses, so it's not a surprise I've ended up being a grower.

What are the main challenges you face as a grower?

Dealing with constantly changing outside weather conditions makes every day different. Even though we have the controlled climate of the greenhouse, we have to adjust how it works in line with the conditions outside. Other factors like the volatility of the energy markets, legislation and meeting the needs of our customers make the job unpredictable and pretty challenging.

What's the best thing that's happened to the British pepper growing industry in the last 10 years?

Well, seeing as Thanet Earth only came into operation in 2009, I have to say that Thanet Earth is the best thing that's happened to the industry in that time! We've managed to bring a large increase to the amount of peppers grown here in the UK, helping

to reduce the reliance on imports and answer the shopper demand for more locally grown food.

What's next for pepper growing?

We're always on the lookout for interesting new varieties – peppers that might be a little sweeter or provide something different for shoppers. We have great connections with seed houses, which are driving much of this innovation. With their help, we get to be 'first to market' with new ideas.

Tangmere Airfield Nurseries

'When it comes to peppers, you never know what you might see next on the supermarket shelves'

Meet... Gerard Vonk, general manager of Tangmere Airfield Nurseries
Located... Chichester, West Sussex
Growing area... 75 acres
Amount grown... 60 million bell peppers, including Tangmere's own special variety of pointed pepper
Pepper experience... 23 years
Favourite pepper recipe... Loves the simplicity of tray roasting peppers with olive oil

How did you first get into pepper growing?

My father was also a grower, so it's in my blood! I was practically grown in a glasshouse myself, as my mother was still working in our family nursery the morning of the day I was born, and by the afternoon there I was! I grew up in Holland, but moved to West Sussex to help set up the nursery, and we've now been growing peppers exclusively for the past 23 years.

Why did you choose to grow peppers?

Sweet peppers are a very exciting product to grow, as there are so many possibilities of growing different shapes and sizes. The fact that we now have more than 30 different varieties at the nursery just goes to show.

What makes Chichester the best place to grow peppers?

Located in West Sussex between the South Downs and the sunny south coast, the old airfield site is well situated for growing peppers, as our crops benefit from the mild climate.

Which is your favourite pepper?

The red bell pepper varieties are satisfying to grow and great to eat!

What are the main challenges you face as a grower?

The weather plays a large part in the success of pepper crops. Poor light levels and cold weather can impact on yields and quality. Besides this, fuel costs mean we have to seek out energy saving measures that offer both economic and environmental benefits to reduce our inputs. Other challenges include discovering we have a new pest or disease in the crop and finding natural solutions to combat them. Growers work really hard to use their skills and the tools at their disposal to do what is best for the crop.

What's next for pepper growing?

The pepper has become an established fruit with the shoppers at home, however there is still plenty of scope to convert even more people to eating peppers. In this industry you never stop learning and you can't stand still. We are always looking for new ways of selling peppers and growing with less input. We work closely with seed companies to trial new varieties and shapes, so you never know what you might see next on the supermarket shelves.

LEA VALLEY GROWERS

'I hope to see the introduction of LED lights so we can harvest for 12 months of the year'

Meet... Gary Taylor, managing director of Lea Valley Growers
Located... Valley Grown Nursery, Essex
Growing area... 10 acres
Amount grown... 6 million Californian Wonder blocky peppers, mini sweet and pointed peppers
Pepper experience... 15 years
Favourite pepper recipe... Puppy breath chilli (page 70)

What's the best thing about growing peppers?

They are a very clean crop, which doesn't attract that many pests in comparison to other salad products. Also, in comparison, it is not too labour intensive.

Why do you grow peppers in Essex?

We are located 12 miles north east of London and historically this is because of its closeness to the capital and the London markets.

Which is your favourite to eat and which is your favourite to grow?

The mini sweet or the Italian long pointed peppers are my favourite to eat and the blocky Californian types are a pleasure to grow.

What are the main challenges you face?

As growers, the things we are most concerned with are the weather, how to get good labour, afford energy prices and get through all that government red tape.

What's the best thing that's happened to the British pepper growing industry in the last 10 years?

The best thing that has happened for me is the shift in consumer perception of peppers as a culinary tool. There has been an increased use of peppers in cooking, and not just as a raw product, as well as the uptake of the niche peppers coming to market.

What's next for pepper growing?

I think we are going to see more automation in the industry, as well as the introduction of LED lights so we can harvest for 12 months of the year. I'd also like to see an increase in greener energy and fertilizers on the market.

Index

Bread
    Beef and pepper bunny chow 96
    Fried squid with romesco sauce and pepper
        croutons 93
    Hearty meatballs 61
    Red pepper damper bread 90
    Roasted lamuyo pepper with chorizo and
        garlic toast tapas 99

Cheese and dairy
Cream
    Beef stroganoff 74
    Chilli and red pepper chocolate mousse 66
    Chilli hot chocolate 40
    Fillet steak with pepper cream sauce 97
    Orange pepper cheesecake 58
Cheese
    Barbecued pepper melts 36
    Chicken and pepper risotto 73
    Goat's cheese, walnut and chicory salad with
        yellow pepper dressing 46
    Herby pepper and halloumi kebabs 33
    Orange pepper cheesecake 58
    Pepper, aubergine and goat's cheese tart 62
    Red pepper and cream cheese cupcakes 59
    Red pepper, feta and mint muffins 52

Chocolate
    Chilli and red pepper chocolate mousse 66
    Chilli hot chocolate 40

Couscous
    Roasted pepper couscous 33

Fish and seafood
    Fried squid with romesco sauce and pepper
        croutons 93
    Jambalaya 64
    Pan-fried seabass with pepper and paprika
        sauce 35
    Rare tuna 'au poivre' and piperade tapas 100
    Roasted lamuyo pepper with chorizo and
        garlic toast tapas 99
    Seafood and peppers in black bean sauce 86
    Sweet pepper salmon 27
    Thai green crab curry 72

Fruit
Apples
    Berry and red pepper smoothie 39
Apricots/dried
    Lamb sosaties 76
Avocados
    Hot guacamole 38

Bananas
    Berry and red pepper smoothie 39
Lemon
    Berry and red pepper smoothie 39
    Chicken and pepper risotto 73
    Herby pepper and halloumi kebabs 33
    Pepper, aubergine and goat's cheese tart 62
    Pepper balti 56
    Rare tuna 'au poivre' and piperade tapas 100
    Red pepper, lemon and coriander
        focaccia 98
Lime
    Hot guacamole 38
    Spicy tofu and noodle soup 41
    Thai green crab curry 72
    Thai turkey and pepper stir-fry 32
    Vietnamese pepper salad 28
Orange
    Brazilian black bean soup 54
Raspberries/strawberries
    Berry and red pepper smoothie 39

Herbs
Basil
    Chilli hot chocolate 40
    Herby pepper and halloumi kebabs 33
Coriander
    Pepper balti 56
    Red pepper, lemon and coriander
        focaccia 98
    Stuffed padron peppers (Bharela Marcha) 89
    Thai green crab curry 72
    Thai turkey and pepper stir-fry 32
    Vietnamese pepper salad 28
Mint
    Roast pepper couscous 34
    Vietnamese pepper salad 28
Oregano
    Hearty meatballs 61
Parsley
    Beef stroganoff 74
    Chicken and pepper risotto 73
    Jambalaya 64
    Sweet pepper salmon 31
Rosemary
    Salsa salu 45
Thyme
    Barbecued pepper melts 36
    Pepper, aubergine and goat's cheese tart 62

Meat and poultry
Beef

Beef and pepper bunny chow 96
Beef and pepper Wellington 80
Beef stroganoff 74
Fillet steak with pepper cream sauce 97
Hearty meatballs 61
Puppy breath chilli 70
Steamed Vietnamese stuffed peppers 42

Chicken
Chicken and pepper risotto 73
Jambalaya 64
Madagascar chicken 65
Steamed Vietnamese stuffed peppers 42

Lamb/mutton
Lamb sosaties 76
Moroccan mutton and pepper tagine 85
Scottish pepper, potato and black pudding breakfast stack 88
Seared lamb, lentil and roasted red pepper salad with salsa verde 91

Sausage/chorizo
Beef and pepper bunny chow 96
Chorizo, yellow pepper and basil penne 43
Jambalaya 64
Roasted lamuyo pepper with chorizo and garlic toast tapas 99
Scottish pepper, potato and black pudding breakfast stack 88
Sweet potato, roasted pepper and chorizo loaf 82

Turkey
Thai turkey and pepper stir-fry 32

Nutmeg
Pan-fried seabass with pepper and paprika sauce 35

Pasta
Chorizo, yellow pepper and basil penne 43
Red pepper pasta 75
Spicy tofu and noodle soup 41

Peanuts
Vietnamese pepper salad 28

Pine nuts
African sunrise salad 69
Roast pepper couscous 34

Pink peppercorns
Red pepper damper bread 90
Sweet pepper salmon 31

Potatoes
Scottish pepper, potato and black pudding breakfast stack 88

Rice
Chicken and pepper risotto 73

Squash and pepper stacks 92

Vegetables
Aubergine
Pepper, aubergine and goat's cheese tart 62
Bean sprouts
Thai turkey and pepper stir-fry 32
Black beans
Brazilian black bean soup 54
Seafood and peppers in black bean sauce 86
Steamed Vietnamese stuffed peppers 42
Broccoli
Mini pepper and vegetable tempura with sweet chilli sauce 84
Rare tuna 'au poivre' and piperade tapas 100
Capers
Mixed pickled peppers 50
Carrot
Brazilian black bean soup 54
Hearty meatballs 61
Salsa salu 45
Vietnamese pepper salad 28
Celery
Jambalaya 64
Sweet pepper salmon 31
Chickpeas
Roasted pepper couscous 33
Courgette
Hearty meatballs 61 Herby pepper and halloumi kebabs 33
Mini pepper and vegetable tempura with sweet chilli sauce 84
Thai turkey and pepper stir-fry 32
Cucumber
Vietnamese pepper salad 28
Garlic
Brazilian black bean soup 54
Chicken and pepper risotto 73
Hearty meatballs 61
Hot guacamole 38
Jambalaya 64
Mixed pickled peppers 50
Pan-fried seabass with pepper and paprika sauce 35
Pepper, aubergine and goat's cheese tart 62
Pepper balti 56
Roasted tomato and red pepper relish 60
Salsa salu 45
Spicy tofu and noodle soup 41
Thai green crab curry 72
Thai turkey and pepper stir-fry 32
Vietnamese pepper salad 28
Ginger
Pepper balti 56
Spicy tofu and noodle soup 41
Thai green crab curry 72

Vietnamese pepper salad 28

Lentils
Seared lamb, lentil and roasted red pepper
salad with salsa verde 91

Mushrooms
Beef and pepper Wellington 80
Beef stroganoff 74
Chicken and pepper risotto 73
Spicy tofu and noodle soup 41

Olives
Roasted tomato and red pepper relish 60
Salsa salu 45

Onion
Barbecued pepper melts 36
Beef stroganoff 74
Brazilian black bean soup 54
Chicken and pepper risotto 73
Jambalaya 64
Salsa salu 45

Onion, red
Herby pepper and halloumi kebabs 33
Pepper, aubergine and goat's cheese tart 62
Thai turkey and pepper stir-fry 32

Shallots
Hearty meatballs 61
Pepper balti 56
Spicy tofu and noodle soup 41
Sweet pepper salmon 31
Thai green crab curry 72

Spinach
Pan-fried seabass with pepper and paprika
sauce 35
Pepper balti 56
Tofu and spinach stuffed pepper curry 94

Spring onions
Roast pepper couscous 34
Spicy tofu and noodle soup 41
Steamed Vietnamese stuffed peppers 42
Vietnamese pepper salad 28

Squash
Squash and pepper stacks 92

Sugar snaps
Thai green crab curry 72

Sweet potato
Beef and pepper bunny chow 96
Sweet potato, roasted pepper and chorizo
loaf 82

Tofu
Spicy tofu and noodle soup 41
Tofu and spinach stuffed pepper curry 94

Tomatoes
Gazpacho 47
Herby pepper and halloumi kebabs 33
Hot guacamole 38
Jambalaya 64
Peperonata 71

Pepper balti 56
Roasted tomato and red pepper relish 60
Salsa salu 45
Virgin pepper Mary 44

Skills
Blanching 22, 38

Bread making 90, 98

Chicken stock 65

Cook a steak 97

Make pasta 75

Melting chocolate 66

Poach an egg 88

Prepare squid 93

Puff pastry 81

Quarter a chicken 65

Shortcrust pastry 62